THE
COLLEGE
of
WILLIAM
and
MARY
Williamsburg
Va.

CHAS. M. ROBINSON
ARCHITECTS
RICHMOND, Va.

CHAS. T. GILLET
Landscape Eng'r
Richmond

EX LIBRIS

1618—London Company gives 10,000 acres of land for a University at Henrico.

COLONIAL
ECHO

1928

*1694—Work was begun
on the College Building, what
is now Main Building.*

1723 — BRAFFERTON

BUILDING ERECTED

COLONIAL ECHO
of
PROGRESS

Published by the students of
**WILLIAM AND
MARY COLLEGE**
WILLIAMSBURG, Virginia.
Nineteen hundred &
twenty eight.

DEDICATION

◈

Since the theme of this volume is progress, the staff has chosen for its dedication, one who has, during his association with the college, been the exponent of everything progressive, yet who has at the same time preserved with progress every ideal and tradition from which William and Mary sprang. And so it is with respect, appreciation, and admiration that we dedicate this 1928 edition of the COLONIAL ECHO

to

W. A. R. Goodwin, D.D.

Professor of Biblical Literature and Religious Education and Rector of Bruton Parish Church

1732
The president's house and the college chapel erected.

1859
February 8th, the Main Building was burned.
Rebuilt October, 1859.

FOREWORD

❖

No greater treasure has man on earth than memories, and no sweeter memories exist for one than those centered around his or her college days, and so it has been the aim and purpose of the staff to catch and to instill throughout the general theme of this COLONIAL ECHO the spirits and atmospheres of life at the college in order that these days may be recalled to mind at will by only a glance within its pages. If we fail in realizing our ambitions, we hope that the reader will forgive and realize the gigantic scope of such a task, but if we succeed, we shall feel that our efforts have not been in vain.

John Branch Green
Editor

1865
College reopened in the fall, with Col.
B. S. Ewell as president.

CONTENTS

1921
Jefferson Hall, the first of the New
College Buildings, was opened.

BOARD OF VISITORS

❖

JAMES H. DILLARD . . . . . . *Rector*
GEORGE WALTER MAPP . . *Vice-Rector*

◆

THE VISITORS OF THE COLLEGE

A. H. FOREMAN . . . . . Norfolk, Va.
LULU D. METZ . . . . Manassas, Va.
MISS GABRIELLA PAGE . . Richmond, Va.
DR. F. W. STIFF . . Centre Cross, Va.
JOHN ARCHER WILSON . . Roanoke, Va.
JOHN STEWART BRYAN . Richmond, Va.
JAMES HARDY DILLARD, Charlottesville, Va.
CHARLES J. DUKE . . . . Norfolk, Va.
GEORGE WALTER MAPP . Accomac, Va.
J. DOUGLASS MITCHELL . Walkerton, Va.
HARRIS HART . . . *Member Ex-Officio*
LEVIN W. LANE, JR., *Sec. to the Visitors*

1927
James Barton Rodgers Science
Hall was opened.

THE COLLEGE

THE MAIN BUILDING

Blow Memorial Gymnasium

PHI BETA KAPPA HALL

WILLIAM PRESTON ROGERS SCIENCE HALL

COLLEGE LAKE

THE LIBRARY

The President's Home

The Faculty

Dr. Julian Alvin Carroll Chandler
President

In Memory

of

Dr. John Lesslie Hall

Ph.D., Litt.D., LL.D.

Dean of the Faculty and Professor of English
Language and Literature

Born March 2, 1856

Died February 23, 1928

▼

Member of the faculty of William and Mary from
1888 until 1928, serving the college faithfully and
loyally for forty years.

Faculty

JULIAN ALVIN CARROLL CHANDLER, Ph.D., LL.D.
President of the College

LYON GARDNER TYLER, M.A., LL.D.
President Emeritus

KREMER J. HOKE, M.A., Ph.D.
Dean of the College; Professor of Education

GRACE WARREN LANDRUM, Ph.D.
Dean of Women; Professor of English

WILLIAM T. HODGES, A.M., Ed.D.
Professor of Education

JOHN GARLAND POLLARD, LL.B., LL.D.
Professor of Government and Citizenship; Dean of Marshall-Wythe School of Government and Citizenship

WILLIAM ANGUS HAMILTON, D.C.L.
Dean of School of Economics and Business Administration; Professor of Jurisprudence

VAN FRANKLIN GARRETT, A.M., M.D.
Professor of Chemistry Emeritus

JOSEPH ROY GEIGER, M.A., Ph.D.
Professor of Philosophy and Psychology

DONALD WALTON DAVIS, Ph.D.
Professor of Biology

ROBERT GILCHRIST ROBB, M.A., Sc.D.
Professor of Organic and Analytical Chemistry

ARTHUR GEORGE WILLIAMS, M.A.
Professor of Modern Languages

ROSCOE CONKLING YOUNG, Ph.D.
Professor of Physics

Faculty

EARL GREGG SWEM, A.M., Litt.D.
Librarian

WALTER ALEXANDER MONTGOMERY, Ph.D.
Professor of Ancient Languages

RICHARD LEE MORTON, M.A., Ph.D.
Professor of History

JOSEPH EUGENE ROWE, A.M., Ph.D.
Professor of Mathematics and Director of Extension

WILLIAM A. R. GOODWIN, M.A., B.D., D.D.
Professor of Biblical Literature and Religious Education

L. TUCKER JONES
Professor of Physical Education

LEONA REAVES, B.S., A.M.
Professor of Home Economics

GEORGE WASHINGTON SPICER, Ph.D.
Professor of Political Science

KATHLEEN BRUCE, Ph.D.
Professor of History

EDWARD MOSELEY GWATHMEY, M.A., Ph.D.
Professor of English

GEORGE HOWARD GELSINGER, M.A.
Professor of English and Greek

PAUL ALANSON WARREN, Ph.D.
Associate Professor of Biology

ALBERT F. DOLLOFF, C.P.H.
Associate Professor of Biology

Faculty

CLARENCE M. FAITHFUL, A.B., M.A.
Associate Professor of Psychology

HENRY C. KREBS, M.A.
Associate Professor of Education

HELEN FOSS WEEKS, M.A.
Associate Professor of Education

BEULAH RUSSELL, M.A.
Associate Professor of Mathematics

THOMAS J. STUBBS, JR., A.M.
Associate Professor of History

EUGENE C. BRANCHI, D.N.S., M.A.
Associate Professor of Modern Languages

WILLIAM GEORGE GUY, Ph.D.
Associate Professor of Chemistry

ALFRED WILLIS DEARING, Ph.D.
Associate Professor of Chemistry

WAYNE FULTON GIBBS, B.S., M.S.
Associate Professor of Accounting

LILLIAN A. CUMMINGS, M.A.
Associate Professor of Home Economics

GEORGE EDWARD BROOKS, B.S., B.L.I.
Associate Professor of Public Speaking

FRANK FREDERICK COVINGTON, JR., A.M., Ph.D.
Associate Professor of English

WILLIAM WALTER MERRYMAN, Ph.D.
Associate Professor of Physics

Faculty

SHIRLEY DONALD SOUTHWORTH, Ph.D.
Associate Professor of Economics

WEBSTER SHULTZ STOVER, A.B., B.D.
Assistant Professor of Greek and English

FRED MARTIN THRUN, A.M.
Assistant Professor of Finance

MARTHA ELIZABETH BARKSDALE, A.B., O.D.
Assistant Professor of Physical Education

ALTHEA HUNT, A.B., A.M.
Assistant Professor of English

GRAVES GLENWOOD CLARK, LL.B., B.A.
Assistant Professor of English and Journalism

JAMES DAVID CARTER, Docteur en Droit
Assistant Professor of Modern Languages

CARL A. FRYXELL, M.S., C.P.A.
Assistant Professor of Accounting

CHARLES DUNCAN GREGORY, B.S., M.A.
Assistant Professor of Mathematics

JAMES RUSSELL PATE, M.A., Ph.D.
Assistant Professor of Government

ALBION GUILFORD TAYLOR, A.M., Ph.D.
Associate Professor of Economics

DUDLEY WARNER WOODBRIDGE, J.D.
Associate Professor of Jurisprudence

MERRILL PROCTOR BALL
Instructor in Piano, Voice, and Harmony

Faculty

EMILY MOORE HALL, A.B., A.M.
Instructor in English

JOSEPH C. CHANDLER, B.S.
Instructor in Physical Education

MARTHA HOLLIDAY, B.S.
Instructor in Home Economics

MARGUERITE WYNNE-ROBERTS
Instructor in Physical Education

OLIVE WILLARD DOWNING, A.B., A.M.
Instructor in Biblical Literature and Religious Education

MRS. KATHLEEN HIPP
Instructor in Music

BEATRICE I. SELLEVOLD, B.S.
Instructor in Fine Arts

FLOYD JAY BAILEY, Sc.M., in E.E.
Instructor in Mathematics and Industrial Arts

ISABEL BRUGADA
Instructor in Modern Languages

GLADYS CALKINS, M.A.
Instructor in Mathematics

GEORGE E. GREGORY, M.A.
Instructor in English

ADELAIDE B. JOHNSON, A.M.
Instructor in Art

MARY GLADYS OMOHUNDRO, B.S.
Instructor in Biology

JOHN C. POOLE, A.B.
Instructor in Modern Languages

 THE CLASSES

Graduate Students

MARIE EVELYN HOFMEYER
Applicant for Master of Arts Degree

EULA ANNE MASSEY
Applicant for Master of Arts Degree

WILLIAM GUY NEAL
Applicant for Master of Arts Degree

GEORGE MARION NOLLEY
Applicant for Master of Arts Degree

ELSIE LEE MASSEY
Applicant for Master of Arts Degree

RUTH LILLEY
Applicant for Master of Arts Degree

Graduate Students

HERBERT L. GANTER
Applicant for Bachelor of Laws Degree

LUCY MERIWEATHER MORGAN
Applicant for Master of Arts Degree

MARJORIE B. OBER
Applicant for Master of Arts Degree

H. CRIS SOMERS
Applicant for Bachelor of Laws Degree

THOMAS PATRICK WALSH
Applicant for Bachelor of Chemistry Degree

CONWAY H. SHIELD, JR.

ZELDA X. SWARTZ

SARAH WINFREE DARLING

The Seniors

WILLIAM HENRY ELLIOTT, JR.

A.B.

NORFOLK, VIRGINIA

President Senior Class

Theta Delta Chi; Omicron Delta Kappa; Phi Delta Gamma; Phi Delta; Sophomore Tribunal;
President Philomathean Literary Society, '27; Collegiate Debate Team; Manager Debate Council;
Captain Freshman Basketball, '25; Varsity Football, '26-'28.

WOODLEY J. BLACKWELL
B.S.

FOLLY, VA.

Alpha Kappa Psi; Beta Alpha Psi; Manager Track, '28; Athletic Council, '28; Varsity Club.

WILLIAM BIRCH BOLTON
A.B.

FRIES, VA.

Alpha Psi; Inter-Collegiate Debate Team, '28-'29; Inter-Fraternity Council, '28; Manager Wrestling, '28; Inter-Collegiate Debate Council, '28; Vice-President Phoenix Literary Society, '28; Y. M. C. A. Cabinet, '28; Phi Delta Gamma; Kappa Phi Kappa; Cotillion Club; Square and Compass.

THOMAS GUY BURKE
B.S.

CUMBERLAND, MD.

Sigma Alpha Epsilon; Cotillion Club; Secretary-Treasurer, '28; Inter-Fraternity Council, '28, Vice-President, '28; Thirteen Club; Assistant Manager Football, '25.

TINSLEY CARTER HARRISON
A.B.

HAMPTON, VA.

Sigma Alpha Epsilon; Inter-Fraternity Council, '28.

ANNIE MILDRED BOZARTH
A.B.
WILLIAMSBURG, VA.

Chi Alpha; J. Leslie Hall Literary Society;
Music Club; Y. W. C. A.; Glee Club; Art
Club.

KATHERINE FITZSIMMONS
A.B.
ZELIONOPLE, PA.

Chi Alpha; J. Leslie Hall Literary Society;
Art Club; Music Club; Y. W. C. A.

FITZ ORMOND CLARK
B.S.

CHURCH ROADS, VA.

Sigma Nu; Wyth Law Club; Thirteen Club;
Cotillion Club; President Inter-Fraternity
Council, '28; President Athletic Association,
'28; Varsity Baseball Squad, '27-'28; Tennis
Team, '26-'27.

WILLIAM C. LINN
B.S.

NORFOLK, VA.

Sigma Nu; Editor-in-Chief Colonial Echo,
'28; Manager Basketball, '28; Inter-Fraternity Council, '26-'27-'28; F. H. C. Society;
Omicron Delta Kappa; "B. B." Club; Athletic Council, '27-'28; Cotillion Club.

KATHLEEN EMILY CONE
A.B.

HURON, S. D.

Y. W. C. A. Cabinet; Art Club; Glee Club;
German Club; Vice-President Barrett Hall,
'28; Huron College.

NORMA AILEEN DORAN
B.S.

NORFOLK, VA.

J. Leslie Hall Literary Society; Corcoran
Scholarship, '27; Edward Coles Scholarship,
'28; Kappa Delta Pi; Pi Gamma Mu.

ALICE CARY CHEWNING
B.S.

ORANGE, VA.

Kappa Kappa Gamma; G. G. G.; German
Club; H-2-E; Varsity Hockey, '25-'26-'27;
Manager Hockey, '27; Monogram Club;
Vice-President Junior Class; President Jef-
ferson Hall, '28; Colonial Echo Staff, '28;
Judicial Council, '28; J. Leslie Hall Literary
Society.

FRANCES THOMSON
A.B.

GOODE, VA.

Kappa Kappa Gamma; K. O. B.; Debate
Council; Secretary German Club, '28; President Pan-Hellenic Council, '28.

MARTHA ROMAYNE CLAIBORNE
A.B.

ASHLAND, VA.

Delta Chi Delta; Freshman Representative
Honor Council; Y. W. C. A.; German Club;
Assistant Art Editor Colonial Echo, '26;
Art Editor, '28; J. Leslie Hall Literary So-
ciety; Dramatic Club; Art Club, Secretary,
'27.

MARTHA LOWRY HALE
A.B.

ELK CREEK, VA.

J. Leslie Hall Literary Society; Y. W. C. A.;
German Club; Varsity Basketball Squad,
'25-'26.

ELIZABETH E. DUKE
A.B.

CHURCHLAND, VA.

Kappa Alpha Theta; G. G. G.; Glee Club;
German Club; Basketball Squad, '25-'26-'27-
'28; J. Leslie Hall Literary Society; Art
Club; President Athletic Association, '28;
Fire Chief, '27.

LOIS HARRIET EVANS
A.B.

CORAL GABLES, FLA.

Kappa Alpha Theta; German Club; G. G. G.;
Los Quixotescos.

DOROTHY VAUGHN FARRAR
B.S.

FARMVILLE, VA.

Kappa Alpha Theta; Edith Baer Club; G.
G. G.; German Club; Art Club; Vice-President Glee Club; Glee Club Shows, '26-'27-'28;
Co-ed Minstrels, '25; Class Historian; Freshman Commission, '25.

RUTH CONSTANCE JAMES
B.S.

RICHMOND, VA.

Kappa Alpha Theta; Alpha Club; German
Club; G. G. G.; Secretary-Treasurer Freshman Class; Student Government Council,
'26-'27-'28; President Barrett Hall, '28; Glee
Club Shows, '26-'27-'28; Co-ed Minstrel, '26;
President Glee Club, '27; Judge Supreme
Court, '27; Varsity Hockey Squad, '27;
Freshman Commission, '24.

HENRY CRIGLER
B.S.
MADISON, VA.
Sigma Pi Sigma; Chi Beta Phi; Kappa Delta
Pi.

HENRI CHASE
A.B.
KILMARNOCK, VA.

JAMES ALLAN COOKE
A.B.

PETERSBURG, VA.

Theta Delta Chi; President Student Body,
'28; Honor Council, '26-'27-'28; Vice-President, '27; President Sophomore Class; Senior-Junior Council; Vice-President Y. M. C.
A., '27; Omicron Delta Kappa; F. H. C. Society; Varsity Football; Varsity Club; Spanish Club; Freshman Basketball Team, '25.

WILLIAM G. THOMPSON
B.S.

NORFOLK, VA.

Theta Delta Chi; Omicron Delta Kappa;
Alpha Kappa Psi; Beta Alpha Psi; President
Honor Council; Manager Baseball, '28; 3-3-3
Athletic Committee; Athletic Council; Manager Freshman Football, '28; Assistant Manager Basketball; Secretary-Treasurer Sophomore Class; Editor Student Handbook, '27;
Y. M. C. A. Cabinet, '27-'28.

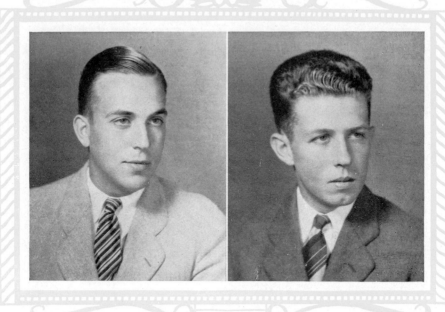

TERRY CROSSFIELD
B.S.

BIRMINGHAM, ALA.

Kappa Alpha; Freshman Basketball, '25;
Freshman Baseball, '25; Tennis Team; Manager, '27; Captain, '28; Cotillion Club; Alpha Kappa Psi; Varsity Basketball Squad, '27;
Vice-President Cotillion Club, '28.

WILLARD C. JAMES
A.B.

IRVINGTON, VA.

Kappa Alpha; Editor-in-Chief "Flat Hat"
'28; Tennis Team; Manager, '28; Freshman Baseball, '25; Cotillion Club; Sigma Upsilon;
Phi Delta Gamma; "Minus Mary," '27.

HELEN LOUISE HOSTETLER
A.B.

DES MOINES, IA.

Kappa Alpha Theta; University of Southern California, '24, '25; Drake University, '25, '26, '27; Glee Club, '27, '28; J. Leslie Hall Literary Society, '27, '28; German Club; K. O. B.; Zeta Phi Eta; Dramatic Club, '27, '28.

VIRGINIA FLOYD
A.B.

LYNN, MASS.

Kappa Alpha Theta; K. O. B.; German Club; Art Club; J. Leslie Hall Literary Society; Debate Council, '25, '26; Second Vice-Presilent of Women's Student Government, '26, '27; President German Club, '26, '27; President Art Club, '27, '28; President K. O. B., '27, '28; Girls' Minstrel, '24-'25, '25-'26; Glee Club Show, '26-'27, '27-'28.

JAMES M. EASON
B.S.

SOUTH NORFOLK, VA.

Phi Kappa Tau; Omicron Delta Kappa;
Vice-President Student Body, '27-'28; Varsity Club; Freshman Tribunal, '25-'26; Varsity Football, '25, '26, '27; Varsity Baseball, '26, '27, '28; Captain, '28.

E. P. SIMPKINS
A.B.

RICHMOND, VA.

Phi Kappa Tau; Secretary Phoenix Literary Society, '26; Vice-President Phoenix, '26; History Club; Kappa Phi Kappa; Cotillion Club; Pi Gamma Mu; Eta Sigma Phi; Y. M. C. A. Cabinet, '27, '28.

R. R. JONES
B.S.
DILLWYN, VA.

Phi Delta Gamma; Phoenix Literary Society; Chaplain '26; Secretary and Treasurer, '26, '27; President, '27.

WALTER ALBERT PORTER
B.S.
MONARAT, VA.

Theta Chi Delta; Chi Beta Phi; Kappa Phi Kappa; Phoenix Literary Society, '25, '26, '27, '28; Megaphone Club, '25, '26, '27, '28; Biology Club, '26, '27, '28; Captain Rifle Team, '26; Member Band, '26, '27.

MAURY WELDON THOMPSON
A.B.

RICHMOND, VA.

Sigma Phi Epsilon; Omicron Delta Kappa; Kappa Phi Kappa; Chi Beta Phi; Kappa Delta Pi; Phi Delta Gamma; Inter-Fraternity Council; Cotillion Club; DeMolay Club; Dramatic Club; Inter-Collegiate Debate Team, '26-'27-'28; President Debate Council, '27-'28; Phoenix Literary Society; Y. M. C. A. Cabinet, '26-'27-'28; Flat Hat Staff, '26-'27-'28; Associate Editor Flat Hat, '26; Editor-in-Chief Straw Hat, '27; Editor-in-Chief Indian Handbook, '27.

CHARLES HAYDEN RUSSELL
B.S.

GREENBUSH, VA.

Sigma Phi Epsilon; Alpha Kappa Psi; Kappa Phi Kappa; Phi Delta Gamma; Wythe Law Club; Glee Club; Minstrels, '25-'26-'27; "Colonial Echo" Staff, '26-'27-'28; Summer School Dramatics, '27; Flat Hat Staff, '27; Straw Hat Staff, '27; Junior Class Poet, '27; Men's Musical Comedy, '26-'27-'28; Phoenix Literary Society.

MAY BARRY REILLY
A.B.

HAMPTON, VA.

Flat Hat Staff, '25; Los Quixotescos; Vice-
President, '28; Kappa Delta Pi; J. Leslie
Hall Literary Society; Glee Club; Hockey
Squad, '27.

DORIS RATHIEN
A.B.

ETTRICKS, VA.

Kappa Delta Pi; Eta Sigma Phi; J. Leslie
Hall Literary Society; Y. W. C. A.; Clayton-
Grimes Biology Club.

SARAH MARIE HUGHES
A.B.
NORFOLK, VA.

J. Leslie Hall Literary Society; Y. W. C. A.;
Gibbons Club; Eta Sigma Phi.

ELEANOR RANDOLPH FORD
A.B.
WOODSTOCK, VA.

J. Leslie Hall Literary Society; Y. W. C. A.;
Art Club; Beechwood School.

ALFRED ZACHRY WILLIAMS

WILLIAMSBURG, VA.

SENIOR LAW STUDENT

Lambda Chi Alpha; Wythe Law Club; Varsity Club; Member Virginia Bar; Inter-Fraternity Council, '26-'28; Secretary Inter-Fraternity Council, '27-'28; American Legion; Overseas Club; Judge Supreme Court, '27; Varsity Football, '21, '22, '25, '26.

FLOYD A. GESSFORD

B.S.

WASHINGTON, D. C.

Lambda Chi Alpha; Glee Club, '25, '26; Minstrels, '24, '25, '26; Flat Hat Staff, '27; Alpha Kappa Psi; Delta Mu Chi.

M. C. DAVIS
B.S.

NORFOLK, VA.

Sigma Alpha Epsilon; Omicron Delta Kappa; Sigma Delta Psi; Thirteen Club; Athletic Committee, '25-'26; Vice-President Honor Council, '27-'28; Varsity Football, '24-'25-'26-'27, Captain, '27; Varsity Basketball, '24-'25-'26-'27, Captain, '27; Varsity Track, '26-'27-'28, Captain, '28; Sophomore Tribunal, '25-'26; Inter-Fraternity Council; President Varsity Club, '27-'28; Chairman Senior-Junior Council, '27-'28; Cast First Musical Comedy, "Minus Mary."

DONALD KEACH VAN WORMER
A.B.

SLINGERLANDS, N. Y.

Sigma Nu; Omicron Delta Kappa; Flat Hat Club.

THELMA RIXEY STINNETT

A.B.

REMINGTON, VA.

Kappa Delta Pi; Y. W. C. A.; Treasurer J. Leslie Hall Literary Society; Art Club; House Vice-President; Graves Scholarship, '25-'26; Joseph E. Johnston Scholarship, '26-'27; Corcoran Scholarship, '27-'28.

MYLDRED LIEBRECHT

A.B.

PORTSMOUTH, VA.

G. G. G.; Kappa Delta Pi; Varsity Basketball Squad; Art Club; Y. W. C. A.; J. Leslie Hall Literary Society.

HENRY BALL
A.B.

DAVENPORT, VA.

Phi Kappa Tau; Theta Chi Delta; Kappa
Phi Kappa; Art Club; Treasurer of Art
Club; Phoenix Literary Society.

GEORGE ALLAN WATTS
B.S.

NEWPORT NEWS, VA.

Biology Club, '27-'28; Laboratory Assistant
Biology, '27-'28.

ELIZABETH PAXTON LAM
A.B.

NORFOLK, VA.

Freshman Commission, '25; History Club;
Y. W. C. A., Secretary, '26-'27, President,
'27-'28; Women's Student Government Ex-
ecutive Council, '26-'27, ex-officio member of
Executive Council, '27-'28; Delegate to State
Y. W. C. A. Conference, '27; Life Saving
Corps; J. Leslie Hall Literary Society; Ger-
man Club; Delegate to Southern Y. W. C. A.
Conference, '26, '27; Delegate to National
Student Conference, Milwaukee, '27; Alpha
Club.

LOIS EDITH LANE
B.S.

HAMPTON, VA.

MELBA MAYHEW GRAVELY
A.B.

RICHMOND, VA.

G. G. G. Club; German Club; Eta Sigma Phi;
Pi Gamma Mu; Kappa Delta Pi; Y. W. C.
A. Cabinet, '27-'28.

HAYDEN GWALTNEY
A.B.

SPRING GROVE, VA.

Y. W. C. A.; State Teachers College, Har-
risonburg; J. Leslie Hall Literary Society;
Kappa Delta Pi.

S. ASHTON OZLIN
B.A.
KENBRIDGE, VA.
Kappa Phi Kappa.

HUGH STALEY
B.S.
RURAL RETREAT, VA.

E. JEANETTE WARD
A.B.

NEWPORT NEWS, VA.

Eta Sigma Phi; J. Leslie Hall Literary Society, '25, '26, '27; Y. W. C. A., '25.

ALENE WALKER
A.B.

BINNS HALL, VA.

Kappa Delta Pi; Los Quixotescos; J. Leslie Hall Literary Society; Y. W. C. A.

CARRIE CURLE SINCLAIR
B.S.

HAMPTON, VA.

Virginia Intermont College; Columbia University; Hockey Team, '27.

MARION E. LARUE
A.B.

ABINGTON, PA.

Goucher, '24-'26; Glee Club; J. Leslie Hall Literary Society; Y. W. C. A.

META A. RICHARDSON
A.B.
RICHMOND, VA.
Los Quixotescos.

MARY EUDORA THOMAS
A.B.
PORT HAYWOOD, VA.
Los Quixotescos; Honor Roll, '25-'26; Y. W.
C. A.; J. Leslie Hall Literary Society.

HAYDEN CLYDE SMITH
B.S.

PHOEBUS, VA.

Theta Chi Delta; Track Team, '25-'26-'27;
Biology Club, '25-'26-'27; Megaphone Club,
'25-'26-'27; Band, '26-'27.

RANDOLPH N. GLADDING
B.S.

HALLWOOD, VA.

Kappa Phi Kappa; Los Quixotescos; Doc-
tors' Club, '23; Clayton-Grimes Biology Club;
Philomathean Literary Society.

BAUMAN S. MUNDIE
B.S.
CHANCE, VA.

R. WATSON DURHAM
A.B.
BESTLAND, VA.
Varsity Track Team, '23-'24, '26-'28; Varsity
Club.

GERTRUDE HARRIS
B.S.
SEABOARD, N. C.

REBA MILDRED DAMERON
B.A.
DEL RAY, ALEXANDRIA, VA.

J. Leslie Hall Literary Society; Y. W. C. A.;
Music Club, '25, '26, '27.

LEONA DUBRAY
A.B.

DUPREE, S. D.

J. Leslie Hall Literary Society.

JUDITH ALICE KERR
B.A.

HAMILTON, VA.

Eta Sigma Phi; Los Quixotescos; J. Leslie
Hall Literary Society.

EDWARD HARVIE HILL
B.S.

DEWITT, VA.

Theta Chi Delta; Phi Delta Gamma; Clayton-Grimes Biology Club; Megaphone Club; Phoenix Literary Society, Secretary, '27, Vice-President, '27, Sergeant-at-Arms, '26.

JAMES GASKINS, JR.
B.S.

SUNNY BANK, VA.

Kappa Phi Kappa.

LOUISE RICE
A.B.

PHOENIX, VA.

Kappa Delta Pi; Eta Sigma Phi; J. Leslie
Hall Literary Society, '25-'26; Y. W. C. A.,
'25-'26-'27-'28; Glee Club, '27-'28.

EMMA HESTER WARING
A.B.

BROOKLYN, N. Y.

J. Leslie Hall Literary Society; Y. W. C. A.;
W. and M. Summer School in Europe, '25;
Université de Toulouse, Institute Normale,
'25-'26, Faculté des Lettres, '26, Université
de Paris, '27; Art Club, '27-'28; Los Quixotescos, '27-'28.

MARY ELNA SPITLER
B.S.

LURAY, VA.

Transfer from W. M. C.; Y. W. C. A., '26;
White Hall Literary Society; Edith Baer
Club; K. O. B.

IOLA VIRGINIA JOHNSON
A.B.

PORTSMOUTH, VA.

Glee Club; K. O. B.; J. Leslie Hall Literary
Society; Graduate State Teachers College,
Farmville, Va.

NOMA ELIZABETH FUQUA
B.S.
RADFORD, VA.

Alpha Chi Omega; Whitehall Literary Society; Y. W. C. A.; Glee Club; Dramatic Club; Pan-Hellenic Council, '26-'27-'28; German Club.

PHYLLIS FAUNT LEROY HUGHES
B.S.
WEST POINT, VA.

Alpha Chi Omega; Freshman Commission, '25; Edith Baer Club; Alumnae Secretary. '25-'26; Program Chairman, '27-'28; Y. W. C. A.; J. Leslie Hall Literary Society.

MARGARETTE SWEENEY
B.S.

RICHMOND, VA.

Phi Mu; German Club; G. G. G.; Art Club;
Freshman Debate Training Class; Debate
Council, '28; Inter-Collegiate Debate Team,
'28.

ELSIE STEWART WEST
A.B.

NEWPORT NEWS, VA.

Glee Club; Vice-President Art Club, '27-'28.

WILLIAM CURTIS WEST
B.S.

ONANCOCK, VA.

F. H. C. Society; B. B. Club; Thirteen Club;
Wythe Law Club; President Cotillion Club,
'27-'28; Inter-Fraternity Council, '27-'28;
Business Manager Literary Magazine, '27-
'28; Y. M. C. A. Cabinet, '25-'26; Assistant
Manager Baseball, '26-'27.

LAWRENCE W. I'ANSON
A.B.

PORTSMOUTH, VA.

Pi Kappa Alpha; Flat Hat Club Society;
Omicron Delta Kappa; Wythe Law Club;
Business Manager Flat Hat, '27; Flat Hat
Staff, '25-'28; President Y. M. C. A., '27;
Manager Cross-Country, '27; Orator's Medal
Freshman Contest, '24; Assistant Manager
Track, '24-'27; Inter-Fraternity Council;
Carr Memorial Cup Committee; Secretary
Phoenix Literary Society, '25; Delegate Na-
tional Y. M. C. A. Conference, Milwaukee,
Wis.; Cotillion Club.

JOHN BRANCH GREEN
A.B.

SURRY, VA.

Kappa Alpha; Cotillion Club; Varsity Club;
Varsity Track; Relay Team; "Colonial Echo"
Staff; Sports Editor, '27, Associate Editor,
'28; "Flat Hat" Staff, Sports Editor, '27;
Alumni Editor, '28; Vice-President Y. M. C.
A., '28; Y Cabinet, '28; Glee Club; "Minus
Mary," '27; Monogram Show, '28; Editor-
in-Chief Colonial Echo, '28; Omicron Delta
Kappa; Sigma Upsilon.

L. M. ANDERSON
A.B.

CRAMERTON, N. C.

Kappa Alpha; Captain Freshman Baseball,
'25; Freshman Football, '26; Inter-fraternity
Council, '28; Cotillion Club; Phoenix Literary Society.

MARY RIBBLE
A.B.

RICHMOND, VA.

Kappa Alpha Theta; German Club; G. G. G.;
Y. W. C. A. Cabinet; Art Club; "Flat Hat"
Staff, '27; Associate Editor, '28; Vice-President Jefferson Hall, '28; Glee Club.

FLORENCE RUTH HARRINGTON
B.A.

DES MOINES, IOWA

Kappa Alpha Theta; Transfer Drake University; German Club; K. O. B.; Art Club;
Y. W. C. A.

WILLIAM EDWARD BOZARTH
B.S.

WILLIAMSBURG, VA.

Theta Delta Chi; Alpha Kappa Psi; Wythe
Law Club; President College Band, '25, '26,
'27; Rifle Team, '25; Music Club; Williamsburg Club; Cotillion Club.

S. NELSON BROWN
B.S.

SCHLEY, VA.

Phi Kappa Tau; Kappa Phi Kappa; Phoenix
Literary Society; Y. M. C. A., '26-'27.

VIRGINIA CHRISTIAN FARINHOLT
A.B.

WEST POINT, VA.

Kappa Kappa Gamma; Art Club; Glee Club;
German Club; K. O. B.; President J. Leslie
Hall Literary Society, '28; Art Staff "Colon-
ial Echo," '28.

CHRISTINE LANTZ
B.S.

DELAND, FLA.

Chi Omega; K. O. B.; Y. W. C. A.; Edith
Baer Club; Art Club; German Club; J. Leslie Hall Literary Society.

WILLIE SHELTON
A.B.

CHATHAM, VA.

Alpha; Eta Sigma Phi; G. G. G.; German
Club; Y. W. C. A. Cabinet, '28; Treasurer
and Vice-President J. Leslie Hall Literary
Society; Flat Hat Reporter; Inter-Collegiate
News Editor, '28; Monogram Club; Varsity
Hockey; Track; Archery; Baseball; R. C.
Life Saving Corps.

DOROTHY BROUGHTON
A.B.

PORTSMOUTH, VA.

K. O. B.; J. Leslie Hall Literary Society;
Y. W. C. A.; Art Club; German Club.

J. LOGAN HUDSON
B.S.

PORTSMOUTH, VA.

Alpha Psi; Track Team, '25-'26-'27; Cross-
Country Team, '24-'25-'26; Captain Cross-
Country, '26; Varsity Club; Kappa Phi Kap-
pa; Sigma Pi Sigma; Chi Beta Phi; Band;
Inter-Fraternity, '27.

ROBERT EMERSON BEELER, JR.
A.B.

PENNINGTON GAP, VA.
Lambda Chi Alpha; Alpha Kappa Psi.

MARGUERITE GENE MILES
A.B.

Phi Mu; H-2-E; Varsity Basketball, '25-'26-
'27-'28; Captain Basketball, '28; Varsity
Hockey Team, '26-'27; Whitehall Literary
Society; Monogram Club.

ETTA HOWERTON CLEMENTS
A.B.

LEE HALL, VA.

Chi Alpha; Eta Sigma Phi; Y. W. C. A.

JOHN R. L. JOHNSON, JR.
A.B.
EAST RADFORD, VA.

RAYMOND DRISCOLL
B.S.
TOANO, VA.

STANLEY H. POWELL
B.S.
PORTSMOUTH, VA.
Sigma Pi Sigma.

STANLEY A. FEIN
A.B.
BROOKLYN, N. Y.
Phoenix Literary Society; Declamation
Medal, '26; Manager Rifle Team, '25; Captain Rifle Team, '26; Inter-Collegiate Team,
'27; Dramatics, '27.

FRANCES E. HUNT
A.B.

PORTSMOUTH, VA.

German Club; Glee Club; Assistant Manager Basketball; J. Leslie Hall Literary Society; Art Club; Clayton-Grimes Biology Club; Y. W. C. A.

MARY C. HUNT
A.B.

PORTSMOUTH, VA.

German Club; Glee Club; Art Club; J. Leslie Hall Literary Society; Assistant Manager Basketball; Clayton-Grimes Biology Club; Y. W. C. A.

HELEN L. MOORE
A.B.

SPARTA, VA.

J. Leslie Hall Literary Society.

KATHERYN MAE TOPPING
A.B.

NEWPORT NEWS, VA.

Chi Alpha; Eta Sigma Phi; Los Quixotescos; Debate Team, '26-'27-'28; Debate Council, '27-'28; Chaplain J. Leslie Hall Literary Society, '28; Art Club; Y. W. C. A.; Honor Council, '27-'28; Hiking Club; President Brown Hall, '28; Pan-Hellenic Council, '28; Judicial Council, '28; Sophomore Tribunal, '26.

HANNAH MARGOLIS
B.A.

NEW YORK, N. Y.

Phi Sigma Sigma; Chi Delta Phi; Pi Gamma
Mu; Chi Delta Phi; Associate Editor Lit-
erary Magazine, 1926-'28; Literary Magazine
Poetry Prize, 1927; Essay Prize, 1927; J.
Leslie Hall Literary Society; Biology Club;
Secretary, 1927; Class Poet, 1928.

RUTH STERN
B.A.

RICHMOND, VA.

J. Leslie Hall Literary Society.

RAY POOLE
B.A.
VICTORIA, VA.

Kappa Phi Kappa; Manager Swimming Team, 1927-'28; Poet Freshman Class, 1924-'25; Virginia Historical Society; Dramatic Club; Monogram Club Show, 1924-'26; Freshman Tribunal, 1925-'26; Assistant Cheer Leader; Glee Club; Phoenix Literary Society; Megaphone Club; College Band.

GEORGE THOMAS MORECOCK
B.S.
PORTSMOUTH, VA.

Beta Alpha Psi; Square and Compass; Business Manager Straw Hat, 1927; Associate Editor Hand Book; Secretary-Treasurer Student Body, 1927-'28; Treasurer Y. M. C. A., 1927-'28; DeMolay Club; Philomathean Literary Society; "Flat Hat" Staff, 1924-'25.

MARJORIE D. LACY
A.B.

SCOTTSBURG, VA.

Pi Beta Phi; Chi Delta Phi; Alpha; German
Club; G. G. G.; Y. W. C. A. Cabinet, '28;
"Flat Hat" Staff, '27; Hockey Squad, '27;
Vice-President Senior Class; Secretary-
Treasurer Pan-Hellenic Council, '28.

RUTH HAZEL SAUNDERS
A.B.

SOUTH HILL, VA.

Pi Beta Phi; G. G. G.; German Club; J.
Leslie Hall Literary Society; Freshman
Commission, '26; Hockey Squad, '27.

ELIZABETH M. JOHNSON
B.A.

NORFOLK, VA.

Y. W. C. A.; J. Leslie Hall Literary Society;
Vice-President Tyler Hall, 1925-'26; Secre-
tary Executive Council, 1926-'27; President
Music Club, 1926-'27; Chairman Freshman
Committee, 1927-'28.

LEILA FRANCES GORDON
B.S.

APPOMATTOX, VA.

Pi Gamma Mu; Alpha Club! Freshman Com-
mission, 1925; Y. W. C. A. Cabinet, 1926-
'28; Judicial Council, 1926-'27; Executive
Council, 1927-'28; Clayton Grimes Biology
Club; Delegate Y. W. C. A. Conference Blue
Ridge, 1927.

CATHERINE COOPER REARDON
B.A.
ALEXANDRIA, VA.
J. Leslie Hall Literary Society; Y. W. C. A.

ELIZABETH NICHOLAS
B.A.
DAYTON, OHIO
Delta Chi Delta; Los Quixotescos.

LILLION CASSELL
A.B.
AUSTINVILLE, VA.

LENA VIRGINIA WALDROP
B.A.
CARDWELL, VA.

J. Leslie Hall Literary Society; Monogram
Club; Hockey Team; Baseball Team; Hiking
Club; Y. W. C. A.

CARROLL VERNON
B.A.
PIRKEY, VA.
Cross Country Team, 1925-'27; Track, 1926-
'28; Wrestling Team, 1928.

T. B. HALL
B.A.
KILMERNOCK, VA.

MATTIE ELIZABETH WALKER
B.A.
RICHMOND, VA.

ANNA HENDERSON
A.B.
WILLIAMSBURG, VA.

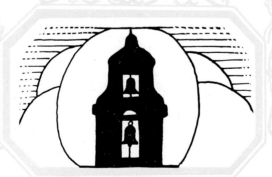

ELIZABETH A. GLENN
B.S.
RICHMOND, VA.
Y. W. C. A.; J. Leslie Hall Literary Society;
Glee Club, 1927-'28.

LIBBIE PAULINE COGLE
B.S.
DISPUTANTA, VA.
Edith Baer Club; Y. W. C. A.; J. Leslie
Hall Literary Society.

MARY WALL CHRISTIAN
A.B.
WILLIAMSBURG, VA.

LUCILE FOSTER
B.A.
WILLIAMSBURG, VA.

Kappa Delta; Pi Gamma Mu; Kappa Delta
Pi; Virginia History Prize, 1926-'27; Student
Assistant in German, 1927.

MARGARET BRANCH
A.B.
TOANO, VA.

DOROTHY DICKENSON BUNDY
B.A.
LEBANON, VA.

German Club; Y. W. C. A.; J. Leslie Hall
Literary Society; Los Quixotescos.

WILLIAM BARKSDALE ATTKISSON
B.A.

RICHMOND, VA.

Sigma Pi Sigma; Kappa Phi Kappa; Y Cabinet; Glee Club 1926-'28; Virginia Historical Society; Phoenix Literary Society; Music Club; College Band, 1924-'25; Monogram Club Show, 1926-'27; Track Squad, 1925; Football Squad, 1926.

E. D. REYNOLDS
B.S.

CHATHAM, VA.

LAURA S. WHITEHEAD
B.A.

CHATHAM, VA.

Chi Omega; G. G. G.; German Club; Judicial Council, 1926-'27, President, 1927-'28; First Vice-President Student Government, 1927-'28; Freshman Commission, 1925-'26; Baseball Team, 1924-'25; Tennis Team, 1925-'28, Manager, 1928; Athletic Council, Secretary, 1925-'26, Treasurer, 1926-'27.

JULIA ELIZABETH SAUNDERS
B.S.

CHESTER, VA.

Chi Omega; Y. W. C. A.; German Club; K. O. B.; Edith Baer Club, Treasurer, 1925-'26; J. Leslie Hall Literary Society.

ANNE WOODLY FIDLER
A.B.

RICHMOND, VA.

Varsity Hockey, '26-'27; G. G. G.; Y. W. C.
A.; German Club; J. Leslie Hall Ltierary
Society; Art Club.

MADOLIN J. WALTON
B.S.

WOODSTOCK, VA.

Chi Omega; Y. W. C. A.; German Club; Glee
Club; Art Club; Edith Baer Club; Vice-
President, '27, Treasurer, '28.

KENNETH B. BEATTY
A.B.

CAPE CHARLES, VA.

Theta Delta Chi; F. H. C. Society; O. D. K.;
7 Society; Dramatic Club; Philomathean
Literary Society; Cotillion Club; "Colonial
Echo" Staff, '25-'26; Advertising Manager,
'26-'27, Business Manager, '27-'28; Y. M. C.
A. Cabinet, '26-'27; President Y. M. C. A.,
'27-'28; Associate Editor Handbook, '26-'27;
Assistant Manager Basketball, '24-'25, '25-
'26; Junior Assistant, '26-'27; Manager
Freshman Basketball, '27-'28; Manager Var-
sity Basketball, second term, '28; Athletic
Council.

GEORGE R. MAPP, JR.
B.S.

MANCHIPONGO, VA.

Theta Delta Chi; Cross Country Team, '25;
Track Team, '25-'26; Alpha Kappa Psi; "Colonial Echo" Staff; Cotillion Club.

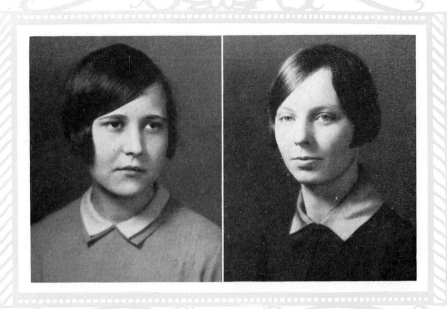

GEORGIA E. SHERRY, B.S.
B.S.
RICHMOND, VA.

Delta Chi Delta; J. Leslie Hall Literary Society; Clayton-Grimes Biology Club; Y. W.
C. A.; Pan-Hellenic Council, '28.

ALICE ELIZABETH CRUTCHFIELD
B.S.
ALTON, VA.

Edith Baer Club; J. Leslie Hall Literary
Society.

ELIZABETH A. SAUNDERS
B.A.

NEWPORT NEWS, VA.

Phi Gamma Mu; Eta Sigma Phi; Kappa
Delta Pi; Los Quixtescos.

MARGARET MURRAY
B.S.

ROANOKE, VA.

EDITH M. HOLLOWELL
A.B.

PORTSMOUTH, VA.

Eta Sigma Phi; Glee Club; J. Leslie Hall
Literary Society; Y. W. C. A.; Girls' Show,
'26-'27.

LENA G. DeSHAZO
B.S.

CENTRE CROSS, VA.

Varsity Basketball, '27-'28, Captain, '28;
Varsity Hockey, '26-'27; Monogram Club;
H-2-E Club; Whitehall Literary Society.

E. BROOKS JOHNSON
A.B.
DREWRYSVILLE, VA.
J. Leslie Hall Literary Society; Music Club,
Art Club; Y. W. C. A.

MARY BULLUCK
A.B.
WILLIAMSBURG, VA.

MANLEY T. MALLARD
B.S.

NORFOLK, VA.

Alpha Psi; Theta Chi Delta; Chi Beta Phi;
DeMolay Club; College Band; Indian Sere-
naders, '27-'28; Freshman Baseball, '25; Instructor in Chemistry.

GRANVILLE C. COX
B.S.

Megaphone Club; Clayton-Grimes Biology
Club; Phoenix Literary Society; Y. M. C. A.

LOWELL C. AYERS
B.S.
WILLIAMSBURG, VA.

Baseball, '26-'27-'28; Theta Delta Chi; Alpha Kappa Psi.

W. M. RINGLAND
B.S.
NORWICH, CONN.

Theta Delta Chi; Kappa Phi Kappa; Philomathean Literary Society; Baseball Squad. '27-'28.

PAGE ROPER DRINKER
B.S.

RICHMOND, VA.

Freshman Representative to Honor Council;
Treasurer Student Government Association,
'26; Representative Judicial Council '26;
Edith Baer Club; President Student Govern-
ment, '26; Alpha Club; Y. W. C. A. Cabinet;
J. Leslie Hall Literary Society; German
Club; Chaplain Junior Class.

MARY MARABLE LAND
A.B.

SURRY, VA.

Kappa Delta Pi; Y. W. C. A.; J. Leslie Hall
Literary Society; Hockey Squad, '25; Freshman, '25; German Club; History Club.

E. CARLTON MACON

B.S.

NORFOLK, VA.

Sigma Phi Epsilon; Omicron Delta Kappa; Alpha Kappa Psi; Sigma Delta Psi; Honor Council, '27; Athletic Council, '28; Varsity Club; Varsity Football, '25, '26-'27; Varsity Basketball Squad, '26-'27; Inter-fraternity Council, '28; Freshman Football, '25; Freshman Basketball, '25; Freshman Track, '26; Treasurer Senior Class; Senior-Junior Tribunal.

EDWIN LEWIS LAMBETH

A.B.

NORFOLK, VA.

Phi Kappa Tau; Phi Delta Gamma; Kappa Phi Kappa; Tau Kappa Alpha; Inter-collegiate Debate Team; Phoenix Literary Society; Assistant Manager Basketball, '25-'26.

RICHARD C. HOWARD
A.B.

NORFOLK, VA.

Tennis Team, '25-'26-'27-'28; Captain, '27; Winner Tournament, '27; Philomathean Society.

ALGERNON K. TURNER
B.S.

DANVILLE, VA.

Lambda Chi Alpha; Omicron Delta Kappa; Sigma Pi Sigma; Theta Chi Delta; Chi Beta Phi; Los Quixotescos; Circulation Manager Literary Magazine, '28; Manager Football, '27; Athletic Council, '28; Inter-fraternity Council, '28; Cotillion Club; Varsity Club; Vice-President Junior Class; President Junior Class.

MILDA B. COHEN
A.B.

NORFOLK, VA.

J. Leslie Hall Literary Society; Women's
Debate Training Class; Eta Sigma Phi.

MARY REBECCA DIGGS
A.B.

SUSAN, VA.

Graduate Farmville State Teachers' College;
J. Leslie Hall Literary Society; Y. W. C. A.

GEORGE E. HUNT
B.S.

QUINTON, VA.

Debate Team, '27-'28; Chairman Y. M. C. A.
Deputation Team; Phoenix Literary Society.

SAMUEL G. DE J. STAPLES
A.B.

NORFOLK, VA.

Phi Delta Gamma; Theta Alpha Phi; Dramatic Club; Art Club; Phoenix Literary Society; Literary Magazine Staff, '27-'28;
"Straw Hat" Staff, '27.

HARRIETTE C. ZIMMERMAN
B.S.

SALEM, VA.

Hockey Team, '24-'25-'26-'27, Captain, '27, Manager, '26; Monogram Club, Treasurer '25-'26-'27; H-2-E Club; Executive Council; Y. W. C. A.; Whitehall Literary Society.

MARY F. SMITHER
A.B.

KILMARNOCK, VA.

Art Club; Y. W. C. A.; J. Leslie Hall Literary Society.

DOROTHY CHALKEY
B.S.
RICHMOND, VA.

Edith Baer Club; G. G. G.; German Club.

MARGARET V. HOWIE
A.B.
NORFOLK, VA.

Alpha Chi Omega; Kappa Delta Pi; Freshman Commission, '26; J. Leslie Hall Literary Society; Y. W. C. A.; Los Quixotescos;
Glee Club; House President Lacy House, '28;
Judicial Council, '28.

MARTHA SLEET
A.B.
NORFOLK, VA.

MIRIAM S. SILBERGER
B.S.
NORFOLK, VA.

J. Leslie Hall Literary Society; Los Quixotescos, President, '27; Manager Women's Debate Council, '27; Y. W. C. A.; Eta Sigma
Phi; Glee Club.

Juniors

JAMES M. ROBERTSON
NORFOLK, VA.

RUTH JONES
FRANKLIN, VA.

PAGE VAUGHAN
ROANOKE, VA.

EDWIN L. TOONE, JR.
BOYDTON, VA.

E. ARMSTRONG SMITH
FARMVILLE, VA.

ELIZABETH SEXTON
BLUEFIELD, VA.

EARNESTINE RENN
PORTSMOUTH, VA.

GEORGE SYER
PORTSMOUTH, VA.

WILLIAM J. STURGIS
NASSAWADOX, VA.

JANE ST. CLAIRE
WEST GRAHAM, VA.

PROGRESS NUMBER

MARGARET BILISOLY
PORTSMOUTH, VA.

CHARLES ARMENTROUT
WAYNESBORO, VA.

WALTER A. COLEMAN
ROANOKE, VA.

INEZ M. BAKER
CARTERSVILLE, VA.

LUCILE CALURA
NORFOLK, VA.

MILTON BLAND
CREWE, VA.

GERALD P. CALLIS
MATHEWS, VA.

MARY B. BLACKMON
CARTERSVILLE, VA.

MILDA B. COHEN
NORFOLK, VA.

THOMAS H. CHRISTIE
NEWPORT NEWS, VA.

PROGRESS NUMBER

NATHAN M. CAFFEE
NORFOLK, VA.

EVA L. ATKINSON
WASHINGTON, D. C.

DOROTHY BOON
ROANOKE, VA.

WILLIAM BEANE
KING AND QUEEN, VA.

JOHN G. AYERS
PUNGOTEAGUE, VA.

ELIZA GEORGE
LOVETTSVILLE, VA.

DORIS CLARKE
RICHMOND, VA.

J. M. HURT
BLACKSTONE, VA.

JOHN W. CLEMENS
LEESBURG, VA.

VIRGINIA HARPER
ROANOKE, VA.

PROGRESS NUMBER

CLARENCE CLEVENGER
GRUNDY, VA.

ANNETTE HUNDLEY
COAN, VA.

MARGARET DIGGS
PORTSMOUTH, VA.

JOHN ERTHERIDGE
WILLIAMSBURG, VA.

BOYD CARTER
DUFFIELD, VA.

MILDRED DUDLEY
BACK BAY, VA.

LAURA FIELDS
NUTTALL, VA.

EDGAR W. KIRBY, JR.
PORTSMOUTH, VA.

WILLIAM MELVIN
CAPE CHARLES, VA.

CHARLOTTE MILEY
ROANOKE, VA.

PROGRESS NUMBER

J. EARNEST NEALE
OPHELIA, VA.

MARGARET L. PAINTER
PULASKI, VA.

VIRGINIA GOULDMAN
FREDRICKSBURG, VA.

H. M. LUDLOW
MORRISONS, VA.

TIVIS D. OWENS
COULWOOD, VA.

SARAH H. PENN
ROANOKE, VA.

ELIZABETH HUNTER
HILTON VILLAGE, VA.

J. ARNOLD MOTLEY
TAPPAHANNOCK, VA.

JAMES O. RICE
REEDVILLE, VA.

MARY G. RIDEOUT
ROANOKE, VA.

PROGRESS NUMBER

DAVID S. MOORE
RICHMOND, VA.

VIRGINIA SMITH
CAPERTON, VA.

LUCILLE PARKER
ROANOKE, VA.

ROBERT PULLEY
PETERSBURG, VA.

B. D. PATTIE
WAYNESBORO, VA.

MARY M. LAND
SURRY, VA.

CATHERINE REYNOLDS
DANVILLE, VA.

JOSEPH N. JAMES
DENDRON, VA.

ERROLL DUNBAR
NEW YORK, N. Y.

ANN TRENT
PORTSMOUTH, VA.

PROGRESS NUMBER

MACON SAMMONS
RICHMOND, VA.

VIRGINIA SMYRE
HAMPTON, VA.

HAWSIE ROWE
BENA, VA.

C. PRESTON SCOTT
MARSHALL, VA.

ALVA D. YEARY
JONESVILLE, VA.

ELIZABETH E. PIERCE
LITWALTON, VA.

VIRGINIA MELTON
FREDRICKSBURG, VA.

CLYDE C. THORPE
WILLIAMSBURG, VA.

JOHN L. LEWIS
BETHESDA, MD.

ISABEL KEMP
NORTON, VA.

120

PROGRESS NUMBER

JULIAN C. CHASE
TARRYTOWN, N. Y.

LYDA MAJOR
STORMONT, VA.

MARY MORRISON
PIGEON, MD.

ROBERT L. COVINGTON
REVIS, VA.

JOHN V. FENTRESS
PRINCESS ANNE, VA.

MAGGIE V. JOHNSON
ZUNI, VA.

MARION LANING
PENNINGTON, N. J.

FREDRICK L. FINCH
NEW YORK, N. Y.

FRANK V. DAVIS
HILTON VILLAGE, VA.

KATHERINE WATSON
MIDDLETOWN, VA.

PROGRESS NUMBER

JOHN S. HINES
IVOR, VA.

BETTY ST. CLAIRE
WEST GRAHAM, VA.

ELIZABETH DUKE
ROANOKE, VA.

CONRAD PIERCE
RECTORTOWN, VA.

JOHN S. OWEN
CLUSTER SPRINGS, VA.

ELIZABETH TANNER
HAMPTON, VA.

REBECCA BALL
ROANOKE, VA.

EDWARD JUSTIS
CHESTER, VA.

C. HOWARD MACMILLAN
BIRMINGHAM, ALA.

DOROTHY SMITHER
NEWPORT NEWS, VA.

PROGRESS NUMBER

EDITH WILKINS
SAN ANTONIO, TEX.

LEE CLAYTON
NEWPORT NEWS, VA.

JAMES F. AYERS
WILLIAMSBURG, VA.

PANSEY HAWLEY
BLUEFIELD, W. VA.

CHARLOTTE ZEIGLER
RICHLANDS, VA.

JAMES A. JOHNSON
MENETA, VA.

GEORGE LAMPROS
NEWPORT NEWS, VA.

MILDRED MAITLAND
ERA, VA.

GRACE VIPOND
NORFOLK, VA.

L. CUSSONS TRICE
TOANO, VA.

PROGRESS NUMBER

CARRIE SHEREN
PORTSMOUTH, VA.

ALVAH HENDLEY
NORFOLK, VA.

GREYSON DAUGHTREY
NORFOLK, VA.

MARGARET HOWIE
NORFOLK, VA.

MARY JOHNSTON
TAZEWELL, VA.

ESTER C. SHORTT
GRUNDY, VA.

ASHLEY LAWERENCE
RICHMOND, VA.

NANCY BURKE
HAMPTON, VA.

MARY RUPP
NEW MARKET, VA.

B. CECIL EMBREY
REMINGTON, VA.

124

WALTER BROOKE
WASHINGTON, D. C.

CHARLOTTE SANFORD
NEWPORT NEWS, VA.

MARJORIE HINEBAUGH
LOWELL, MICH.

ROBERT BARRETT
PORTSMOUTH, VA.

SHELTON PETERS
FRANKLIN, VA.

MARGARET VENABLE
ROANOKE, VA.

LOIS WILSON
CITY POINT, VA.

FRANCES SHEPHERD
CHESTER, VA.

WILLIE ROGERS
FREEMAN, VA.

EDGAR GARRARD
SOUTH BOSTON, VA.

PROGRESS NUMBER

RANDOLPH VAIDEN
NEWPORT NEWS, VA.

MILDRED KIRSNER
HAMPTON, VA.

NANCY B. WARD
TAZEWELL, VA.

AGNES BRITTINGHAM
WACHAPREAGUE, VA.

HELEN GRAVES
BOULEVARD, VA.

GEORGE PORTER
PORTSMOUTH, VA.

LOUISE WHITE
ELIZABETH CITY, N. C.

RHODA M. FRY
HIGHLAND SPRINGS, VA.

RUTH ANDREWS
PHILADELPHIA, PENN.

ROY JOHNSON
CLINCHPORT, VA.

PROGRESS NUMBER

CAMILLA KELLER
WEST POINT, VA.

JAMES H. DEIBERT
NORFOLK, VA.

MARION E. BONNIWELL
HARBARTON, VA.

BARTA WORRELL
RICHMOND, VA.

LOWELL E. HUGHES
BARBOURSVILLE, KY.

LENORE COLEY
FORT MONROE, VA.

HELEN STEINGESTER
BROOKLYN, N. Y.

VIRGINIA BUSTON
TAZEWELL, VA.

MABEL MORTON
REMINGTON, VA.

PARKE H. COX
SURRY, VA.

127

PROGRESS NUMBER

VIRGINIA NICHOLAS
DAYTON, OHIO

ARTHUR HENDERSON
PORTSMOUTH, VA.

OLIVE WIGGLESWORTH
MARYE, VA.

VIRGINIA ALEXANDER
ABINGDON, VA.

JACK GRIZZARD
BRANCHVILLE, VA.

LUCILLE STINNETTE
REMINGTON, VA.

MIRIAM SILBERGER
NORFOLK, VA.

MARGARET BREWER
PULASKI, VA.

RUTH CULTRA
ONARGA, ILL.

JOE HORNBERGER
CHRISTIANSBURG, VA.

PROGRESS NUMBER

HELEN BRISTOW
COMARCHEM, OKLA.

MacLAIN T. O'FERRALL
RICHMOND, VA.

MAXWELL LANIER
WILLIAMSBURG, VA.

POLLY HINES
WASHINGTON, D. C.

FRANCES LEWIS
NEWPORT NEWS, VA.

MILTON STRIBLING
RICHMOND, VA.

JOHN B. HOZIER
NORFOLK, VA.

FRANCES FORD
CARTERSVILLE, VA.

VIRGINIA HANNA
ROCHESTER, VA.

ROBERT VAUGHAN
STEVENSVILLE, VA.

PROGRESS NUMBER

HELEN K. JOHNSON
FRANKLIN, VA.

J. HUGH NELSON
NEWPORT NEWS, VA.

PHYLLIS LOGAN
NORFOLK, VA.

REED WEST
CREWE, VA.

LOUIS ROTGIN
NORFOLK, VA.

J. R. ADDINGTON
GATE CITY, VA.

LLOYD WILLIAMS
NORFOLK, VA.

CATHERINE RHODES
MIDDLETOWN, VA.

SALLY B. FARMER
JETERSVILLE, VA.

GENEVIEVE HOFMAN
WHITE PLAINS, N. Y.

130

PROGRESS NUMBER

Sophomores

Sophomore Class

OFFICERS

Y. O. KENT . . . . *President*

ROBBIE YEATES . . . . *Vice-President*

ELEANOR WILLIAMSON . . . . *Secretary-Treasurer*

CONSTANCE JAMISON . . . . *Poet*

TRUMAN WELLING . . . . *Chaplain*

ELIZABETH VAIDEN . . . . *Historian*

PROGRESS NUMBER

COLONIAL ECHO

Class of 1930

Armistead, Virginia M.
Arthur, Robert
Ashby, Harold G.
Ayers, John Gillet
Babb, B. F., Jr.
Baker, Aileen M.
Bass, Dorothy Vernon
Beebe, Elsie C.
Bell, Frances Elizabeth
Bennett, Mae Afton
Blake, Anne White
Boon, Dorothy Payne
Boswell, Lucy May
Brewster, Lawrence F.
Bridgeforth, E. M.
Briggs, Ether Bernice
Brown, Claude C.
Brown, David S.
Buston, Virginia E.
Cacioppo, Anne
Calhoun, John W., Jr.
Campbell, Gordon E.
Carney, Joseph W.
Carpenter, Susan E.
Casagrande, Stephen R.
Cassell, Lillian Hugh
Charnick, Max
Chase, Julian C., Jr.
Christian, Joe David
Clarke, Amanda M.
Clark, George Paul
Collins, Edna P.
Cooke, Thomas B.
Cornell, Albert
Covington, Harry R.
Crabtree, Marion
Dabney, Florence
Daughtery, Herbert G.
Davies, James Jenkins
Davies, Hawes T., Jr.
Davis, J. Newell
Davis, Melvin C.
Davis, Alyse M.
Davis, Vinnie May
De Falso, Ralph J.
Denison, L. B.
Diggs, Margaret E.
Dillon, Evelyn M.
Dodd, Edith Rae
Doyle, Robert E.
Dubray, Leona M.
Dunbar, Erroll
Dunn, Rosser G., Jr.
Easley, Charles A., Jr.
Edgar, Mary
Ethridge, Bell J.
Ethridge, John
Ely, John
Evans, Edward S.
Everett, Sarah Ann
Fales, Edward D., Jr.
Farmer, Archer D.

Farmer, Leslie S., Jr.
Fentress, Frank L.
Ferguson, Bernice
Fields, William J.
Files, Wilford C.
Finney, Millison
Fleet, Mary Louise
Floyd, Anna Margaret
Folliard, Eugene McK.
Frizzell, Emmet G.
Fulton, Louise B.
Glenn, Dorothy L.
Glenn, F. Berkley
Glenn, Kathryn M.
Glocker, Mary E.
Gold, Norman
Gragg, Eva
Grantham, Robert
Graven, Frank B.
Greenwood, W. M., Jr.
Gresham, Granville
Gresham, Martha G.
Griffin, Frances P.
Gamble, Robert A., Jr.
Garrett, Albert E., Jr.
Garrison, Ellison C.
Hale, Dorothy Ruth
Hall, Margaret L.
Hallam, Eugene S.
Haller, Henry (Miss)
Halpern, Norris E.
Halpern, William
Hancock, H. Jackson
Hancock, Joseph H.
Hanna, Virginia Moat
Hardy, Truly C.
Harrison, James J., Jr.
Harveycutter, Katherine
Harwood, Alice S.
Henley, Alvah M.
Henry, Frances S.
Hicks, Merilla Virginia
Hinebaugh, Margery E.
Hollis, Eldon B.
Holt, Reginald
Hosteteller, Helen L.
Hough, Rose Elizabeth
Howard, Richard C., Jr.
Hughes, Mamie
Hull, Virginia S.
Hunt, George E.
Hurley, Samuel H.
Ironmonger, Thelma
Irwin, Mabel R.
Jackson, Leila
James, Joseph N.
James, Louise Barry
Jamieson, Constance S.
Joerisson, Margaret R.
Johnson, Garland
Johnson, Margaret A.
Johnston, Mary E.

Johnston, Nancy Dupuy
Jones, Clarence P.
Jones, DeEtte
Jones, Mary N.
Jones, Richard J.
Jones, Virginia L.
Keister, Henry C.
Kelly, James B.
Kelsey, Denver A., Jr.
Kent, Yelverton O.
Kerr, Margaret B.
King, Charlotte
Kirsner, Mildred
Lacy, Lois L.
LaForge, Jeanne M.
Lane, Irving Palmer
Lane, Louise
Lanier, Elizabeth W.
Lanier, George M.
Lankford, Dorothy L.
Lavenstein, Lena
Lawson, Irella
LeCompte, Fay P.
Leigh, Joe Riddick
Lewis, John Latane
Lewis, Leon P.
Light, Harry V.
Livingston, Johnson M.
Lovelace, Anna P.
Ludlow, Herbert M.
MacBridge, William G.
MacKay, Alice
McGinn, I. Wanger
McGee, Charles R.
McMillan, Chester H.
Maffet, Helen L.
Mahoney, Archer W.
Mann, Richard
Martin, John H., Jr.
Messick, Anna
Mirmelstein, Samuel H.
Montiero, Helen
Moore, Alva May
Moore, David S.
Moody, Milbry
Moore, Elizabeth T.
Mcrecock, George T.
Morris, Margaret
Morcher, L. N., Jr.
Morton, Helen T.
Morton, Mabel E.
Moses, Robert C.
Motley, Mary L.
Munsey, William
Nash, Beverley W.
Newland, Harold A.
Nicholas, Katheryn
Nicholas, L. Virginia
Nicholson, Betsy R.
Nottingham, Lucy P.
Nofal, George J.
Nolde, John Arthur

PROGRESS NUMBER

Class of 1930

Nuchols, Ryland
Ober, Leroy M.
O'Brien, Albert W.
Owen, Edward
Parker, Edward M.
Pate, William E.
Pattie, Barton Duval
Paul, Cecil V.
Person, Fred R.
Peters, James S.
Phillips, J. W., Jr.
Pilcher, Lucy Duval
Pitts, Mary E.
Pogorelskin, M. D. A.
Poole, Richard Ray
Porter, George P.
Power, Ray C.
Price, Elizabeth W.
Price, Robert P.
Proudman, Alice
Pulley, Robert P.
Quesenberry, Connie G.
Quick, Mary K.
Rabinowitz, Barnard
Repass, Albert Thomas
Reynolds, Emmett D.
Richardson, Joseph M.
Rice, Albert V.
Robben, Herman J.
Rountree, Mattie E.
Rowe, Henry Gordon
Rueger, Louis, Jr.
Rupp, Mary
Rush, Mary F.
Russell, Charles H.
Russell, Lesta M.
St. Clair, Grada
Sanger, Henry M., Jr.
Satterfield, Willow B.

Savage, William R., Jr.
Scammon, Charles F.
Schey, Herman
Schneider, K. L., Jr.
Schofield, Helen L.
Schmutz, George A.
Scott, James E.
Schwertz, Benjamin M.
Shepherd, Frances J.
Shortt, Elster C.
Simpkins, E. P., Jr.
Simmons, Cary L.
Slaughter, J. H., Jr.
Smithers, Mary D.
Smith, E. Armstrong
Smith, Harriet D.
Smith, Clara Ione
Smyre, Sarah M.
Southerland, Daisey
Steele, Evelyn H.
Steingester, Helen C.
Straughn, David H.
Swanson, John Cabell
Synon, George D.
Tankard, Barrand
Tarrango, Gladys
Taylor, Horace P.
Thomas, Robert M.
Thompson, Maury W.
Thorpe, Elizabeth
Todd, R. Gideon
Towler, John P.
Trevillan, Dorothy
Trice, Edward
Trible, Waring
Trout, Mary G.
Tudor, Alice Rae
Turley, John Gouldey
Turman, Virginia
Turner, C. A., Jr.
Usher, Sadie Elizabeth

Urquhart, Alice
Vaiden, Elizabeth
Valentine, Irene G.
Valiska, Albert W.
Van Ausdall, James G.
Van Putten, J. J., III
Varney, Thomas R.
Vaughn, Robert J., Jr.
Vernon, Clifford C.
Vincent, William S., Jr.
Vinyard, William P.
Wallace, James F.
Walrath, Alton
Walters, Edna M.
Ward, John F.
Waring, Emma H.
Warren, Ethel R.
Warren, William E.
Waters, Constance E.
Waters, John H., Jr.
Weaver, Dalmar F., Jr.
Webb, Roselyn
Weiland, Virginia E.
Welling, Truman C.
Werblow, Sol C.
Wheeler, S.
White, Milton G.
Wilcox, Franklin S., Jr.
Wigglesworth, Olive J.
Wilkins, G. F., Jr.
Williamson, Eleanor C.
Wilson, Linda Mae
Winfree, Julia A.
Withers, Robert E., Jr.
Wool, Swain
Worrell, Barta
Wright, Joe V.
Yeatts, Robbie L.
Zehemer, Carey S.

PROGRESS NUMBER

Freshmen

Freshman Class

OFFICERS

WILLIAM SCOTT . . . . *President*

CATHERINE COOK . . . . *Vice-President*

MARGARET FULLER . . . . *Secretary-Treasurer*

WALLACE SMITH . . . . *Chaplain*

FRANCIS THOMPSON . . . . *Historian*

CLAIRE HARGROVE . . . . *Poet*

Class of 1931

Abbott, Meredith W.
Adams, Irma R.
Addis, Alice A.
Allen, Mary E.
Ambler, Elizabeth L.
Anderson, Janey P.
Anderson, John C.
Anderson, Raymond R.
Arnold, Regina B.
Ashmend, Anita
Austin, Patsy
Bailey, Margaret
Baldacci, Paul
Balderson, Randolph
Ballard, Edward
Balmanne, Dorothea
Baltz, Elizabeth
Banks, Jewell
Baker, Sue
Barrett, Viola
Bauserman, John
Bayliss, Wyllhart
Beale, Lloyd
Beard, Frank
Beebe, Vernette
Bennett, Joe
Berkman, Oliver
Berry, Calvin
Berry, Evelyn
Bidwell, Lucille
Blackwell, Elizabeth
Blair, William
Blanke, Ethel
Booker, C. L.
Bowen, William
Bowman, James
Bradshaw, Hersey
Bradshaw, Wilber
Brame, Mildred
Brewington, Norman
Broadwater, William
Brooks, Sallie
Brown, Iva
Bruce, Harriett
Bryant, Thelma
Bunch, Catherine
Burgwyn, Bartlett
Burgwyn, Frances
Burke, Lucille
Butler, Everett
Butt, Matthew
Butte, Clarence
Caddy, Herbert
Camp, Junius
Campbell, Horace
Carmichael, W. E.
Carter, Ralph
Carter, Tunis
Carver, Edwina
Cassidy, Fred
Caulk, Octavia
Chambers, John
Chandler, Charles

Channing, L. C.
Chaplin, Margaret
Charles, Roy
Charnock, Calvin
Chewning, John
Cheynie, Marian
Chick, Florence
Childress, Peyton
Christian, Margaret
Christensen, G.
Clarke, Alma M.
Clarke, Bernard
Cleveland, George
Colter, Roger
Coddington, W. W.
Colburn, Edna
Cole, Walter
Coley, Lenore
Collins, Russell
Comess, William
Cook, Catherine
Cooper, John
Cook, Clarice
Copenhaver, Charles
Coppola, Andrew
Cornelius, William
Cornick, Frances
Costantino, A. E.
Cochran, Catherine
Cox, Albert
Crawford, Lucy
Close, Byron
Crigler, Frances
Crigler, Virginia
Crockett, Doris
Currier, Jane
Curry, Earnest
Curtis, Naomi
Darden, Frank
Davis, Carrie
Davis, Bryan
Davis, Irwin
Davis, Sherman
DeBartini, Walter
Diffin, Margaret
Doran, Raymond
Douglas, Betty
Duggar, William
Dunlap, Elizabeth
Dunlap, Mary W.
Dunnington, Robert
Early, John
Eckstein, Harry
Edwards, Rodger
Eggleston, Anna
Eichelberger, William
Ellis, Fendall
Ellis, Margaret
Ellison, James
Elmore, Clarence
Enfield, Robert
Ennis, Alma

Epaminonda John
Erwin, Elizabeth
Etheridge, Julian
Everhart, Rosa
Farinola, Gerald
Farmer, Sally B.
Ferguson, Jeter
Ferrandini, Ralph
Ferrall, William
Fink, Joseph
Fitch, Mary
Flippen, Oliver
Fitchett, Margaret
Floyd, Fluvana
Foley, John
Forbes, Mattie
Ford, Antonia
Foster, Geraldine
Fowler, Harry
Frost, William
Fuller, Margaret
Gay, Pettus
Garrard, Clarence
Gilbert, Eugene
Gilley, James
Glascock, Robert
Glenn, Channing
Goods, Thornton
Goodwin, Norvelle
Gough, Isabel
Graham, James
Graves, Kenneth
Green, Lucy
Greenberg, Margaret
Griffin, Elizabeth
Griffin, James
Garnett, Robert
Garnett, James
Habel, James
Hailey, Charles
Hale, Ethel
Haley, L. J.
Haley, Mary
Holligan, Dorothy
Hall, Cecil
Hall, Irma
Hamilton, Philip
Hammontree, Gladys
Hancock, Corrine
Handy, Marion
Hargrove, Clare
Harris, Garland
Harrison, Mildreth
Harrison, Marian
Hart, Emmett
Hawley, Blythe
Hayman, Francis
Hasseltine, Catherine
Haynes, Evelyn
Haynie, William
Hayward, Albert
Healy, Elliott

Henderson, Gertrude
Hennion, Ted
Higgins, Thomas
Hicks, Wallace
Hilder, Lillion
Hilliard, Caroline
Hogge, Helen
Holland, Griffin
Holland, Marvin
Holmes, Alice
Hopkins, Jesse
Howard, E. K.
Hubbard, James
Hudson, William
Hugo, Elizabeth
Hunt, James
Hunter, Katherine
Irby, Robert
Iromongar, Batelle
James, Thomas
Jameson, John M.
Johnson, Albert
Johnson, Georgia
Johnson, Harry
Johnson, R. Terrall
Jones, Curle L.
Jones, Roberta
Jones, Gladys
Joyce, Ewell
Joyner, Upshur
Joyner, William
Kahle, Katherine
Katz, Moyer
Kaufman, Julius
Keay, Roger
Kelly, Charles
Kelley, Mildred
King, Agnes
King, Ollie
Kirk, Albert
Kistler, Hughes
Lam, Katherine
Land, Kermit
Lanford, Carrie
Langhorne, Nan
Langford, Sam
Lawson, William
Leach, Edward
LeKites, Katherine
Levin, Orrin
Levy, Cecelia
Lewis, Harold
Lindsey, Anne
Lipman, Rheba
Little, Ethel
Little, Peyton
Larenzen, Helen
Lowe, Esther
Lucy, James
Lukin, Frank
MacKinnen, Gorden
McAnally, Eugene

PROGRESS NUMBER

Class of 1931

MacDonough, Charles
McElroy, Katherine
McGinnis, Margaret
McKann, Homer
McKown, Charlotte
McRae, John
Maier, Dorothy
Mann, Conklin
Marshall, Margaret
Marshall, Philip
Massey, Costelle
Mayhew, Mary
Melfi, Domenick
Mears, Hilton
Montzer, Mary
Miller, Martha
Miller, Hilda
Miller, Lucy
Moore, Ann
Morris, Edward
Morton, Lucy
Moss, Virginia
Mozeleski, Mitchell
Mullen, Marian
Mullowney, Richard
Munden, James
Murphy, James C.
Murphy, James W.
Neale, Evelyn
Nelson, Harry
Nelson, John
Nelson, Virginia
Nightengale, David
Novitte, Richard
Newbill, Hugh
New, John
Nesselrodt, Maude
Ninninger, Mary
Niven, Charles
Nolde, Rudolph
Norton, Paul
Novick, Edward
Nuckols, Muriel
Nunn, Ethel
O'Brien, Paul
Oden'hal, Sarah
O'Neil, William
Orange, Irma
Orbach, Sylvia
Overstreet, Moulton
Padgett, Weymouth
Page, Constance
Pannill, Robert
Parker, Kelvin
Parker, Emma
Parker, Peggy
Parker, William
Parsons, Ellen
Paxson, B. F.
Payne, Carrie
Pendleton, Catherine
Pendleton, Kenneth
Perdue, Lewis
Massey, Mildred
Matthews, Betty
Philips, Alden
Phillips, Lester
Pierce, Blanche
Pierce, Gibson
Pifer, Helen
Pilcher, Louise

Pitt, Charles
Poole, Arnold
Pope, Thomas
Porter, Chester
Porter, Helen
Powell, Elizabeth
Powell, Walker
Powell, Meredith
Powell, William
Pretlow, William
Powers, Helen
Price, Betsy
Prillaman, Page
Railey, John
Rand, James
Reeve, Esther
Reese, Dorothy
Reid, Amy
Reinach, Ellis
Renshaw, William
Rhinestein, Samuel
Rhodes, Dorothy
Ribble, Alice
Richardson, Edith
Richardson, Hampton
Rice, Roy
Ricketson, Elliott
Riddick, Emmett
Riddle, Benjamin
Rittenburg, Nathan
Rives, Clarence
Robertson, Mary
Robinson, Lavinia
Roach, Edward
Rose, Tina
Rountree, William
Rowe, Edna
Ruffin, John
Rux, Julian
Ryder, Everett
Ryland, Elizabeth
Salasky, Milton
Sandidge, Hobson
Sanders, Linda
Sergent, Charles
Sergent, Marion
Scott, William
Scully, Jack
Seaman, Ruth
Sencindiver, Mary
Seward, Kathryn
Shepherd, Edgar
Shirley, Genie
Shoemaker, Joseph
Shreves, Melvin
Schucker, Louise
Shultz, Gladys
Siegfried, John
Silverman, Abraham
Sindele, Victor
Simpson, Edmund
Skora, Olga
Slater, Mildred
Slemp, Lena
Slemp, Margaret
Slough, Louise
Smither, Bettie
Smith, Barney
Smith, Bula
Smith, Earnest

Smith, Eleanor
Smith, George
Smith, Morris
Smitth, Pauline
Smith, Russell
Smith, Waller
Smith, William
Snow, Charles
Snider, J. K.
Spicer, Bernard
Spicer, Herbert
Spindle, Fannie
Spital, Nellie
Steinback, Joseph
Stewart, Herbert
Stewart, Robert
Stokes, Louise
Stone, James
Stone, Lois
Story, William
Stradley, Sherner
Strayer, Jack
Streeter, Kenneth
Stubbs, Archie
Suttle, Oscar
Swan, Elizabeth
Swats, Donald
Swem, Earl
Swift, Pauline
Taylor, Clarence
Taylor, Cornelia
Sauerbrun, John
Saunders, Vincent
Savedge, John
Savage, James
Savage, Martha
Thacker, Josephine
Thomas, Fred
Thomas, James
Thomas, Max
Thomson, Christine
Thompson, Francis
Thompson, Ralph
Ticer, Ellen
Tillage, Robbie
Titiev, Matthew
Trabold, Vera
Trevilian, W. H.
Trotter, Leigh
Trout, Elizabeth
Tudor, Mary
Toone, Edwin
Vaccarrelli, Marie
Van Lear, Emily
Vaughan, Eleanor
Waldon, Richard
Wallace, Dorothy
Ward, Mary
Ward, Sarah
Ware, Mary
Waring, Martha
Watkins, Vance
Watkinson, Alma
Way, Elizabeth
Webb, Ewell
West, John
Westbrook, Ruby
White, Carolina
White, Eddie
White, John

White, Stephen
Whitehurst, Indie
Whitlock, Isabelle
Whittemore, Leonard
Wiggins, Edward
Wiley, John
Wilkerson, John
Wilkerson, William
Wilkins, John
Williams, Francis
Williams, Phillip
Williams, Rawlings
Williams, Louis
Williams, Thomas
Williams, Virginia
Willis, Weston
Taylor, Floyd
Taylor, Lucius
Terrell, Robert
Terrell, James
Wimbish, Trixie
Winn, Agnes
Winn, Madeline
Withrow, Clara
Wood, George
Worthington, Jane
Wright, Shirley
Wyatt, Barbara
Wyatte, Genevieve
Wynne, Anne
Yancey, Florence
Yost, Marguerite
Zabel, Rudolph
Zehmer, Richmond
Zeigler, Martha
Zenitz, Lillian

Special Students

Amiel, Henri
Barnes, Robert
Bauserman, R. D.
Brugada, Isabel
Crockett, Paul
Dalton, Dewey
Dalton, Tecumseh
Entwisle, Willard
Fox, Solomon
Hudgins, Kenneth
Irwin, Mary
Keiningham, Thomas
Kerbawy, Edward
Lampros, George
Lane, Emily
Lee, Richard
Lindsley, Pattie
McFarland, Ralph Mrs.
Malcolm, Winfred
Maxey, Landon
Moriarity, George
Moseley, Adolphus
Murphy, Margaret
Porter, Charles
Reynolds, James
Richardson, Dorothy
Rodgers, Arthur
Stone, James
Swingle, Birdie
Trombley, William
Walker, Margaret
Watts, Estelle
Whitehurst, Edna

PROGRESS NUMBER

 **FRATERNITIES**

Interfraternity Council

Theta Delta Chi
W. H. Elliott
W. G. Thompson

Pi Kappa Alpha
Lewis Reuger
Charles Easley

Kappa Sigma
R. W. Roberts
R. C. Power

Sigma Nu
F. O. Clark
D. K. Van Wormer

Lambda Chi Alpha
A. K Turner
Fred Finch

Sigma Alpha Epsilon
T. G. Burke
M. C. Davis

Kappa Alpha
W. N. James
L. M. Anderson

Sigma Phi Epsilon
Weldon Thompson
Hayden Russell

Phi Kappa Tau
E. P. Simpkins
Ed Lamberth

Phi Alpha
Charles Werblow
M. B. Schwetz

Alpha Psi
W. B. Bolton
John Waters

Theta Delta Chi

FRATRES IN FACULTATE

DR. R. C. YOUNG   DR. W. T. HODGES   J. C. CHANDLER

FRATRES IN URBE

R. P. WALLACE   J. WHARBURTON

FRATRES IN COLLEGIO

Class of 1928

WILLIAM H. ELLIOT	. . . . Norfolk, Va.	KENNETH B. BEATTY . . Cape Charles, Va.
LOWELL AYRES	. . . . Williamsburg, Va.	WILLIAM G. THOMPSON . . . Norfolk, Va.
GEORGE R. MAPP	. . . Machipongo, Va.	J. ALLAN COOKE . . . . Petersburg, Va.

Class of 1929

JULIEN C. CHASE	. . . Tarrytown, N. Y.	THOMAS R. VARNEY . . . Alexandria, Va.
ROBERT L. TAYLOR	. . . Petersburg, Va.	W. CAROL BROOK . . Washington, D. C.
MILTON C. STRIBLING	. . . Richmond, Va.	WILLIAM E. BOZARTH . Williamsburg, Va.

Class of 1930

ALTON A. McKANN	. . . Urbanna, Va.	MILTON G. WHITE . . . . Salisbury, Va.
F. SAM WILCOX	. . . Norwich, Conn.	CARY S. ZEHMER . . Newport News, Va.
	GENE FOLLIARD . . . . . Urbanna, Va.	

Class of 1931

ELLIOTT HALEY	. . . . . Saluda, Va.	SEWELL SIMPSON . . . . Richmond, Va.
FRANK DARDEN	. . . . . Norfolk, Va.	FRANCIS HAYMAN . . Princess Anne, Md.
FRANCIS S. THOMPSON	. . . Norfolk, Va.	GRIFFITH HOLLAND . . . . Eastville, Va.
CHARLES CHANDLER	. . . Petersburg, Va.	JOHN ANDERSON . . . . . Keyport, N. J.
WALLACE W. SMITH	. . . Norfolk, Va.	CHARLES PITT . . . . . Portsmouth, Va.
	WILLIAM L. SCOTT . . . Portsmouth, Va.	

Theta Delta Chi was founded in 1847 at Union College. The chapter at William and Mary is the farthest south of all its chapters. Its chapter roll includes 45 chapters, 15 of which are inactive.

The Shield, issued quarterly, is the official magazine.

PROGRESS NUMBER

PROGRESS NUMBER

COLONIAL ECHO

Sigma Alpha Epsilon

Virginia Kappa Chapter

Established 1857

Fratres in Collegio

Class of 1928

Carlton S. Bell	Suffolk, Va.
Thomas G. Burke	Cumberland, Md.
Melvin C. Davis	Norfolk, Va.
Tinsley C. Harrison	Hampton, Va.

Class of 1929

Edward S. Evans	Williamsburg, Va.
David S. Moore	Greenville, N. C.
James S. Peters	Franklin, Va.
James M. Robertson	Norfolk, Va.
LeRoy N. Ober	Norfolk, Va.

Class of 1930

William J. Fields	Baltimore, Md.
William G. MacBride	York, Pa.
Waring Trible	Dunnsville, Va.
John B. Bauserman	Woodstock, Va.
William P. Vinyard	Vinton, Va.

Class of 1931

Everett L. Butler	Lynn, Mass.
Robert D. Bauserman	Woodstock, Va.
Philip T. Marshall	Newport News, Va.
William F. O'Neil, Jr.	South Orange, N. J.
Edward H. Roche	Newport News, Va.
Earl G. Swem, Jr.	Williamsburg, Va.
Robert V. Watkins	Norfolk, Va.
Stephen G. White	Harper's Home, Va.

The Sigma Alpha Epsilon fraternity was founded at the University of Alabama, March 9th 1856. From the beg'nning it was designed to the national in extent and by the end of the year 1857 seven chapters had been established, the last one in William and Mary. Today the organization has 100 active chapters.

The Record is the official publication of the fraternity and appears quarterly.

144

PROGRESS NUMBER

145

Pi Kappa Alpha

FRATER IN FACULTATE
JOHN BUXTON TODD

FRATRES IN URBE

B. E. STEEL   W. L. L. SMOOT   J. C. WALLER

FRATRES IN COLLEGIO

Class of 1928

R. GIDEON TODD	Newport News, Va.
WILLIAM C. WEST	Onancock, Va.
LAWRENCE W. I'ANSON	Portsmouth, Va.
LOUIS RUEGER, JR.	Richmond, Va.
H. G. PARKER	Virginia Beach, Va.

Class of 1929

W. S. BEANE	King and Queen Court House, Va.
WARFIELD W. WINN	Richmond, Va.
HORACE CAMPBELL	Denbigh, Va.
LOWELL HUGHES	Barboursville, Ky.
HENERY R. COVINGTON	Fort Eustis, Va.
A. MONIA WILLIAMS	Williamsburg, Va.

Class of 1930

CHARLES A. EASLEY	Chatham, Va.
JACK J. VAN PUTTEN III	Fort Eustis, Va.
ALTON WALRATH	Fort Plains, N. Y.

Class of 1931

ROY R. CHARLES	Newport News, Va.
W. H. CORNELIUS	Newport News, Va.
CHARLES COPENHAVER	Bristol, Tenn.
GEORGE L. SMITH	Tabb, Va.
JAMES J. RUFFAN	Henrico, Va.
KENNETH STREETER	West Springfield, Mass.
LEONARD WHITTEMORE	Richmond, Va.

Pi Kappa Alpha was founded at the University of Virginia in March, 1868, and has spread throughout the country. At the present time there are seventy-nine chapters listed, of which only nine are inactive.

The official organ is the *Shield and Diamond,* which is issued five times during each college year.

PROGRESS NUMBER

PROGRESS NUMBER

COLONIAL ECHO

Kappa Alpha

FRATRES IN FACULTATE

JULIAN ALVIN CARROLL CHANDLER, B.A., M.A., PH.D., LL.D.
EDWARD MOSELY GWATHMEY, B.A., M.A., PH.D.
WALTER ALEXANDER MONTGOMERY, B.A., M.A., PH.D.
THOMAS JEFFERSON STUBBS, B.A., M.A.
JOHN COCHRAN POOLE, B.A.
LEIGH TUCKER JONES, B.A.

FRATRES IN URBE

REV. JOHN BENTLEY   ASHTON DOVELL

FRATRES IN COLLEGIO

Graduate Student

HERBERT L. GANTER, B.A, Galveston, Tex.

Class of 1928

LEWIS M. ANDERSON . . Cramerton, N. C.	JACOB HENRY FRANTZ, JR. . . Roanoke, Va.
CHARLES TERRY CROSSFIELD, Birmingham, Ala.	WILLARD NEWBILL JAMES . Irvington, Va.
JOHN BRANCH GREEN . . . . Surry, Va.	NORMAH HUFF JOHNSON, JR., Richmond, Va.

MELVIN HOWELL TENNIS, Williamsburg, Va.

Class of 1929

JOHN GUILLET AYERS . . Pungoteague, Va.	THOMAS BUTTE JOHNSON . Gilmerton, Va.
ROBERT SYRE BARRETT . . Portsmouth, Va.	JOHN LATANE LEWIS . . . Bethesda, Md.
MOFFETT HALLEY BOWMAN . Roanoke, Va.	McLAIN T. O'FERRAL . . Richmond, Va.
JETHRO MERIWETHER HURT, Blackstone, Va.	WILLIAM JOSHUA STURGIS, Nassawadox, Va.

EDGAR COLEY GARRARD . South Boston, Va.

Class of 1930

ROGER GREGORY COLTER . . Tunstall, Va.	ROBERT ALLEN GAMBLE . . Petersburg, Va.
THOMAS B. COOKE . Elizabeth City, N. C.	TRULY CRALLE HARDY . . Blackstone, Va.
JOHN EMMETT EARLY . Charlottesville, Va.	DENHAM ARTHUR KELSEY . . Norfolk, Va.
HAWES THORNTON DAVIES, JR., Manassas, Va.	HENRY HOBSON SANDIDGE . . Amherst, Va.
JAMES JENKYN DAVIES . . Manassas, Va.	JOHN WISE WILKINS . . . Onancock, Va.

EDWARD M. BRIDGEFORTH . Kenbridge, Va.

Class of 1931

BARTLETT ROPER BURGWYN . Jackson, N. C.	JAMES WILLIAM MURPHY . . . Surry, Va.
ALBERT EDWARD COX . Spring Garden, Va.	ROBERT SAMUEL PANNILL . Martinsville, Va.
CLARENCE KNIGHT GARRARD, South Boston, Va.	ELLIOTT PERDUE . . . Rocky Mount, Va.
EUGENE K. HOWARD . . . Oxford, N. C.	MEREDITH H. POWELL . Newport News, Va.
ROBERT CANNON IRBY . . Blackstone, Va.	CLARENCE TOMPKINS RIVES . McKenney, Va.

RAWLINGS BAKER WILLIAMS, Portsmouth, Va.

Kappa Alpha was founded at Washington and Lee University in December, 1865, and has extended over the entire south and into California. No chapters exist above the Mason-Dixon line. The fraternity embraces 63 active chapters and has 13 inactive on its rolls.

The official publication is the Journal, issued five times each college session.

148

PROGRESS NUMBER

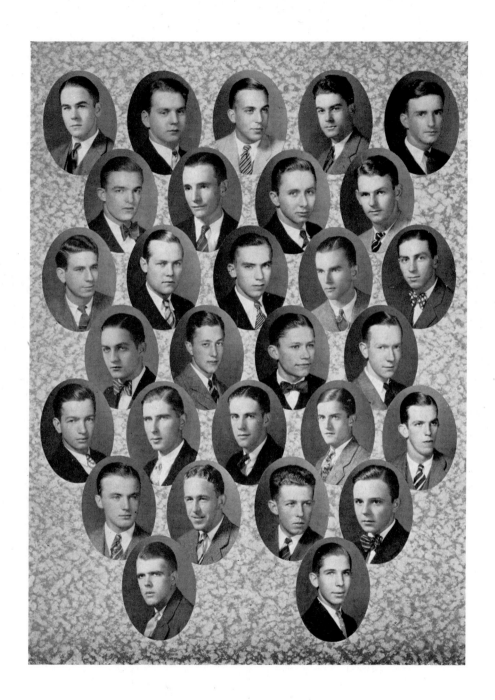

149

Kappa Sigma

NU CHAPTER
Established February 26, 1890

FRATRES IN URBE

VERNON M. GEDDY   EDWARD D. SPENCER
VAN F. GARRETT, JR.   LEVIN W. LANE, III
WILLIAM PERSON   BATHURST D. PEACHY
GEORGE P. COLEMAN   OTIS GEDDY
FIELDING WILSON

FRATRES IN COLLEGIO

Class of 1928

RAYMOND C. POWERS . . . . Follsbee, W. Va.
PAUL L. EVERETT . . . . Holland, Va.
R. WHITFIELD ROBERTS . . . . Richmond, Va.
WILLIAM R. RICHARDSON . . . . Cape Charles, Va.

Class of 1929

JOHN S. OWEN . . . . Cluster Springs, Va.
D. CONRAD PIERCE . . . . Rectortown, Va.
JOSEPH WRIGHT . . . . Keiser, W. Va.

Class of 1930

DELMAR F. WEAVER . . . . Somerset, Va.
FREDERICK R. PERSON . . . . Williamsburg, Va.
NED OWEN . . . . Chase City, Va.
EARNEST A. SMITH . . . . Grundy, Va.

Class of 1931

KIRKMAN SNIDER . . . . Hampton, Va.
SHERMAN STRADLEY . . . . Wilmington, Del.
JACK WHITE . . . . Long Beach, Cal.
WILLIAM A. J. BOWEN . . . . Los Angeles, Cal.
WILLIAM R. PRETLOW . . . . Richmond, Va.

The Kappa Sigma Fraternity was founded at the University of Virginia December 10, 1869. Its growth has been rapid and today its active chapters number 102 while its inactive chapters are 19 in number.

The official organ of the fraternity is *The Caduceus,* published each month for circulation among the members.

PROGRESS NUMBER

PROGRESS NUMBER

Sigma Phi Epsilon

VIRGINIA DELTA CHAPTER
Established 1904

FRATRES IN URBE
J. HILLIS MILLER

FRATRES IN FACULTATE
GEORGE W. REILLY

FRATRES IN COLLEGIO

Class of 1928

JOHN W. CLEMENTS . . . Leesburg, Va.	CHARLES H. RUSSELL . . . Greenbush, Va.
EDWARD C. MACON . . . . Norfolk, Va.	HARRY C. SOMERS . . . . . Bloxom, Va.
MAURY W. THOMPSON . . Richmond, Va.	

Class of 1929

JAMES R. ADDINGTON . . . Gates City, Va.	GEORGE P. PORTER . . . Portsmouth, Va.
NATHANIEL M. CAFFEE . . . Norfolk, Va.	JOSEPH N. JAMES . . . . . Dendron, Va.
ERROLL DUNBAR . . . . New York City	BARTON D. PATTIE . . . . Wynesboro, Va.
JOHN B. HOZIER . . . . . Norfolk, Va.	EDWARD A. SMITH . . . . Farmville, Va.
MACON C. SAMMONS . . . Richmond, Va.	

Class of 1930

IRVIN DAVIS . . . . . . Clarksville, Va.	THOMAS B. POPE . . . Drewrysville, Va.
ROBERT S. DOYLE . . . . Mckenny, Va.	GEORGE SCHMUTZ . . . Youngstown, Ohio
LESLIE FARMER . . . . Elm City, N. C.	DAVIS H. STRAUGN . . . . . Norfolk, Va.
CHARLES M. HAILEY . . . Ontario, Va.	GEORGE D. SYNON . . . . . Norfolk, Va.
YELVERTON O. KENT . . . Norfolk, Va.	TRUMAN C. WELLING . . . . Laurel, Md.
LEON P. LEWIS . . . . . Norwich, Va.	WILLIAM S. VINCENT . . Edenton, N. C.
JOHN A. NOLDE . . . . . Richmond, Va.	HARRY NELSON . . . . . . North, Va.

Class of 1931

JAMES HUNT . . . . . . Oxford, N. C.	ELLIOT G. RICKETSON . New Bedford, Mass.
CHARLES V. MACDONOUGH . Brookline, Mass.	JOHN D. SCHULLY . . E. McKeesport, Penn.
MITCHELL MOZELESKI . . . Camden, N. J.	MELVIN SHREVES . . . . . Bloxon, Va.
FREDERICK R. NOLDE . . . Richmond, Va.	JOHN F. STRAYER . . . . New York City
PAUL W. NORTON . . . . Boston, Penn.	OLIVER T. BERKMAN . . . Monaca, Penn.
ARTHUR G. RODGERS . . Washington, D. C.	ALPHEUS WILSON . . . . Clarksville, Va.
RICHMOND ZEHMER . . . . McKenny, Va.	

Sigma Phi Epsilon was founded at Richmond College (now the University of Richmond), in November, 1901. At the present time active chapters are located at 54 colleges and universities throughout the country and the records show 12 which have existed but are now inactive.

The quarterly periodical is the Sigma Phi Epsilon Journal, which is published in Nebraska.

PROGRESS NUMBER

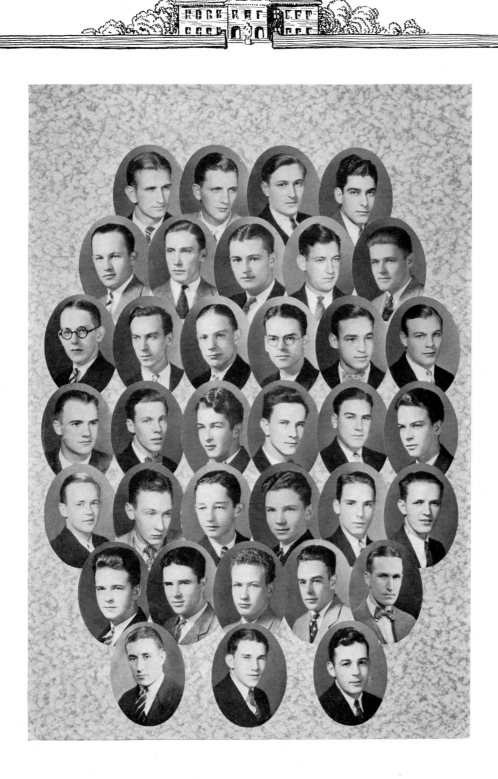

PROGRESS NUMBER

Sigma Nu

Epsilon Iota Chapter
Established December 30, 1921

Frater in Facultate
J. Roy Geiger

Fratres in Collegio

Class of 1928

Fitz Ormond Clarke	Church Roads, Va.
William C. Linn	Norfolk, Va.
Donald K. VanWormer	Slingerton, N. Y.

Class of 1929

George W. Syer	Portsmouth, Va.
Edward L. Toone	Boyton, Va.

Class of 1930

Frank B. Graven	Port Washington, N. Y.
Tecumseh S. Dalton	Pulaski, Va.
Dewey W. Dalton	Pulaski, Va.
Albert Repass	Richlands, Va.
I. Wanger McGinn	West Chester, Pa.
Edward Fales	Schenectady, N. Y.
Stanley Clarke	Church Roads, Va.

Class of 1931

Joseph B. Bennett	Richmond, Va.
Edward S. Leach	Havana, Cuba
Gordon M. McKinnon	Attleboro, Mass.
Richard Mullowney	Brookline, Mass.
Conklin Mann	Pocomoke, Md.
Charles G. B. Niven	Schenectady, N. Y.
Charles F. Porter	Roanoke, Va.
James W. Reynolds	Richmond, Va.
Everett O. Ryder	Pleasantville, N. Y.
Ralph Farrandini	Seattle, Wash.

The Sigma Nu fraternity was founded at the Virginia Military Institute January 1st, 1869. Since that time it has found its way into 105 colleges and universities, in which all but 13 have lived.

The Delta is the official publication of the fraternity and is published quarterly.

PROGRESS NUMBER

COLONIAL ECHO

155

PROGRESS NUMBER

Phi Kappa Tau

Graduate Student

WILLIAM GUY NEAL . . . . Ophelia, Va.

Class of 1928

JAMES AYRES . . . . Williamsburg, Va.
HENRY BALL . . . . Davenport, Va.
S. N. BROWN . . . . Schley, Va.
E. L. LAMBERTH . . . . Norfolk, Va.
E. P. SIMKINS . . . . Richmond, Va.
MERRILL EASON . . . . Norfolk, Va.

Class of 1929

W. E. BLOXSOM . . . . Norfolk, Va.
C. C. BROWN . . . . Schley, Va.
B. G. CARTER . . . . Duffield, Va.
JOHN V. FENTRESS . . . . Princess Anne, Va.
JOS. B. HORNBARGER . . . . Christiansburg, Va.
JOHN E. NEAL . . . . Ophelia, Va.
C. L. SIMMONS . . . . Floyd, Va.

Class of 1930

B. F. BABB, JR. . . . . Ivor, Va.
FRANK L. FENTRESS . . . . Princess Anne, Va.
GEORGE A. MORIARITY . . . . Chateaugay, N. Y.
ROBERT P. PRICE . . . . Martinsville, Va.
JULIAN T. RUX . . . . Crewe, Va.
CHARLES SCAMMON . . . . Newport News, Va.
ROBERT E. STUART . . . . Ivor, Va.
F. JAMES WALLACE . . . . Norfolk, Va.

Class of 1931

WILLIAM FERRELL . . . . Norfolk, Va.
JAMES HABEL . . . . Jetersville, Va.
KENNETH HUDGINS . . . . Petersburg, Va.
WARREN O'BRIEN . . . . Norfolk, Va.
JAMES RAND . . . . Amelia, Va.

Phi Kappa Tau was founded at Miami University in 1906 as a non-Greek letter association, but in 1916, along with the associated organizations, adopted the Greek phrase. The fraternity can now claim 32 chapters, all of which are active.

The Laurel is the official organ and is a quarterly.

PROGRESS NUMBER

PROGRESS NUMBER

Lambda Chi Alpha

Class of 1928

A. Z. WILLIAMS . . . . West Point, Ga.
ALGERNON K. TURNER . . . . Danville, Va.
ROBERT E. BEELER, JR. . . . . Pennington Gap, Va.
FLOYD A. GESSFORD . . . . Washington, D. C.

Class of 1929

GEORGE F. WILKINS, JR. . . . . Long Bottom, W. Va.
FREDRICK L. FINCH, JR. . . . . Brooklyn, N. Y.
EDWARD T. JUSTIS . . . . Chester, Va.
J. L. A. MOTLEY . . . . Tappahannock, Va.
A. D. FARMER . . . . News Ferry, Va.
JOSEPH H. HANCOCK . . . . Newport News, Va.
CHESTER H. MACMILLAN . . . . Moundville, Ala.

Class of 1930

ROBERT ARTHUR, JR. . . . . Fort Monroe, Va.
JOHN C. SWANSON . . . . Danville, Va.
HORACE P. TAYLOR . . . . Danville, Va.
EDWARD M. PARKER, JR. . . . . Emporia, Va.
HARRY C. PAXTON, JR. . . . . Norfolk, Va.

Class of 1931

JULIAN A. ETHERIDGE . . . . Great Bridge, Va.
JAMES M. GILLEY . . . . Big Stone Gap, Va.
KENNEDY GRAVES . . . . Williamsburg, Va.
EMMETT W. HART . . . . Richmond, Va.
GARLAND R. HARRIS . . . . Danville, Va.
CURLE LEE JONES . . . . Hampton, Va.
WILLIAM H. PARKER . . . . Danville, Va.
B. F. WILSON PAXTON . . . . Norfolk, Va.
KENNETH M. PENDLETON . . . . St. Brides, Va.
ROBERT V. TERRELL . . . . Buckner, Va.
WILLIAM A. TROMBLEY, JR. . . . . Buffalo, N. Y.
CALVIN CHARNOCK . . . . Capeville, Va.
JAMES N. GARRETT . . . . Craddock, Va.

Lambda Chi Alpha was founded at Boston University from the Cosmopolitan Law Club in 1909. It is one of the youngest fraternities, yet can boast of an unbroken roll of 73 chapters.

The Purple, Green and Gold is the quarterly publication of the fraternity.

PROGRESS NUMBER

PROGRESS NUMBER

Phi Alpha

Class of 1928

NORMAN GOLD . . . . Rocky Mount, N. C.

Class of 1929

S. CHARLES WERBLOW . . . . Newport News, Va.
LOUIS ROTGIN . . . . Norfolk, Va.
MAX CHARNICK . . . . Harrison, N. J.
SAMUEL JOHN RHINESTINE . . . . New York City

Class of 1930

MOE B. SCHWETZ . . . . Portsmouth, Va.
WILLIAM HALPERN . . . . Norfolk, Va.
NORRIS E. HALPERN . . . . Norfolk, Va.

Class of 1931

HARRY LIGHT . . . . Long Beach, N. Y.
JULIUS KAUFMAN . . . . Long Beach, N. Y.
A. E. SILVERMAN . . . . Hartford, Conn.
S. R. FOX . . . . Norfolk, Va.

Phi Alpha, a fraternity for Jewish students, was founded
in October, 1914, at George Washington University.
The chapter roll for the fraternity numbers 17.
The official publication, Phi Alpha, is a quarterly.

PROGRESS NUMBER

Alpha Psi

FRATER IN URBE
RAY P. EDWARDS

FRATRES IN FACULTATE
RICHARD LEE MORTON   J. D. CARTER   GEORGE E. GREGORY

FRATRES IN COLLEGIO
Class of 1928

J. LOGAN HUDSON	Norfolk, Va.
WILLIAM B. BOLTON	Fries, Va.
MANLEY T. MALLARD	Norfolk, Va.
JOHN S. HINES	Ivor, Va.

Class of 1929

GRANVILLE GRESHAM	Newport News, Va.
LOYD H. WILLIAMS	Norfolk, Va.
CLYDE THORPE	Williamsburg, Va.
ALVAH M. HENLEY	Norfolk, Va.
MAXWELL LANIER	Williamsburg, Va.
IRVING LANE	Newport News, Va.
J. M. RICHARDSON	Churchland, Va.
J. HUGH NELSON	Newport News, Va.

Class of 1930

WILLIAM SAVEDGE	Modest Town, Va.
JOHN H. WATERS	Portsmouth, Va.
JAMES G. VAN AUSDALE	Williamsburg, Va.
JOHN F. WARD	Norfolk, Va.

Class of 1931

J. H. DEIBERT	Norfolk, Va.
JOHN L. WILEY	Portsmouth, Va.
ROBERT F. ENFIELD	Bedford, Penn.
L. R. EDWARDS	Franklin, Va.
J. RICHARD RAILEY	Newsoms, Va.
WILLIAM F. ROUNTREE	Portsmouth, Va.
A. G. MOSELEY, JR.	Newport News, Va.
W. G. PADGETT	Newport News, Va.
SHERMAN DAVIS	Hopeville, Va.

Alpha Psi is a local fraternity organized at
William and Mary in November, 1921.

PROGRESS NUMBER

PROGRESS NUMBER

Chi Omega

SORORES IN COLLEGIO

Graduate Student

LUCY MORGAN	Danville, Va.

Class of 1928

CHRISTINE LANTZ	Deland, Fla.
JULIA SAUNDERS	Chester, Va.
FRANCES SHEPHERD	Chester, Va.
MADOLIN WALTON	Woodstock, Va.
LAURA WHITEHEAD	Chatham, Va.
FRANCES LEWIS	Des Moins, Iowa

Class of 1929

FRANCES SAUNDERS	Newport News, Va.
REBECCA BALL	Roanoke, Va.
KATHERINE HARVEYCUTTER	Roanoke, Va.

Class of 1930

ELSIE BEEBEE	Lewis, Del.
SUSAN CARPENTER	Richmond, Va.
FLORENCE DABNEY	Lynchburg, Va.
EDITH DODD	Montclair, Va.
SARA ANN EVERETT	Holland, Va.
LOUISE JAMES	Washington, D. C.
ALICE URQUHART	Norfolk, Va.
MARY GRACE TROUT	Roanoke, Va.
MARGARET HALL	Washington, D. C.
NAN LANGHORNE	Smithfield, Va.
MARY NININGER	Norfolk, Va.

Class of 1931

ELIZABETH TROUT	Roanoke, Va.
LOIS STONE	Newport News, Va.
ELIZABETH BALTZ	Washington, D. C.
SARA LEE ODENDHAL	Norfolk, Va.
JANE WORTHINGTON	Baltimore, Md.
MARGARET BAILEY	Wilmington, Del.

Chi Omega was organized at the University of Arkansas in 1895. It has the largest chapter roll among the sororities, claiming 76 active chapters and only four that are inactive.

The Eleusis is the official journal of the sorority and is issued quarterly.

PROGRESS NUMBER

Kappa Alpha Theta

Sorores in Collegio

Class of 1928

ELIZABETH DUKE	Portsmouth, Va.
LOIS EVANS	Miami, Fla.
DOROTHY FARRAR	Farmville, Va.
VIRGINIA FLOYD	Lynn, Mass.
FLORENCE HARRINGTON	Des Moines, Iowa
HELEN HOSTETLER	Des Moines, Iowa
RUTH JAMES	Richmond, Va.
MARY RIBBLE	Richmond, Va.

Class of 1929

PHYLLIS LOGAN	Norfolk, Va.
ERNESTINE RENN	Portsmouth, Va.
ELIZABETH SEXTON	Bluefield, W. Va.
LOIS WILSON	City Point, Va.

Class of 1930

VIRGINIA TURMAN	Atlanta, Ga.

Class of 1931

ELIZABETH AMBLER	Warrenton, Va.
VIOLA BARRETT	Alexandria, Va.
HELEN BRISTOW	Oklahoma City, Okla
LUCILLE BURKE	Owensboro, Ky.
DOROTHY BOONE	Roanoke, Va.
IRMA HALL	Onancock, Va.
ESTHER LOWE	State College, Pa.
KATHERINE HUNTER	Whaleyville, Va.
PEGGIE PARKER	Norfolk, Va.
JANE ST. CLAIR	Bluefield, W. Va.
BETTY ST. CLAIR	Bluefield, W. Va.
FLORENCE YANCEY	Marion, N. C.

Kappa Alpha Theta was founded at De Pauw University in 1870 and has the distinction of being the first sorority to bear a Greek letter name and to have principles akin to the men's fraternity. It has 53 active and 11 inactive chapters today.

The publication of the sorority is the Kappa Alpha Theta.

PROGRESS NUMBER

PROGRESS NUMBER

Kappa Kappa Gamma

Sorores in Urbe

Mrs. H. E. Parker   Mrs. W. F. Bozarth

Sorores in Collegio

Class of 1928

Alice Chewning	Orange, Va.
Virginia Farinholt	West Point, Va.
Frances Thomson	Goode, Va.

Class of 1929

Elizabeth Duke	Roanoke, Va.
Virginia Harper	Roanoke, Va.
Page Vaughn	Roanoke, Va.
Margaret Venable	Roanoke, Va.
Marjorie Harris	Washington, D. C.
Katherine Rhodes	Middletown, Va.
Charlotte Sanford	Newport News, Va.

Class of 1930

Constance Jamieson	New York City
Lois Lacy	Richmond, Va.
Dorothy Langford	Princess Anne, Md.
Elizabeth Vaiden	Newport News, Va.

Class of 1931

Virginia Alexander	Abington, Va.
Eva Atkinson	Washington, D. C.
Marian Cheyne	Hampton, Va.
Betty Douglas	Cleveland, Ohio
Marion Handy	Crisfield, Md.
Clare Hargrove	New Haven, Conn.
Anne Lindsey	Richmond, Va.
Virginia Nelson	Norfolk, Va.
Dorothy Rhodes	Middletown, Va.
Christine Thomson	Goode, Va.

Kappa Kappa Gamma made its public appearance at Monmouth College in 1870 and immediately began to expand into other universities and colleges of the country until today there are 63 chapters listed on the rolls. Of these, however, nine are inactive.

The Key is the journal of the sorority and is subscribed to for life by each new initiate.

PROGRESS NUMBER

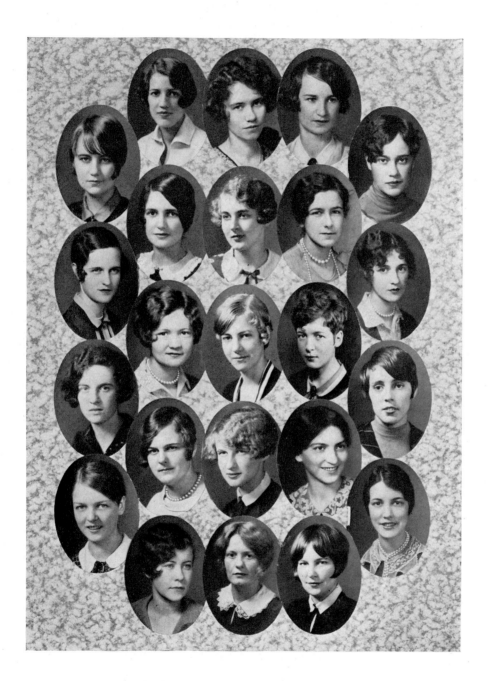

PROGRESS NUMBER

Pi Beta Phi

SORORES IN URBE

ALICE PERSON   CHRISTINE HENDERSON

SORORES IN COLLEGIO

Class of 1928

MARJORIE LACY . . . . Scottsburg, Va.
GRACE MILLER . . . . Dallas, Texas
HAZEL SAUNDERS . . . . South Hill, Va.
ELIZABETH SMITH . . . . Suffolk, Va.

Class of 1929

POLLY HINES . . . . Washington, D. C.
LUCILLE PARKER . . . . Roanoke, Va.
BETSY PRICE . . . . Marlinton, W. Va.
VIRGINIA SMITH . . . . Capron, Va.
ANNE TRENT . . . . Portsmouth, Va.
SUZANNE WHEELER . . . . DeWitt, Iowa

Class of 1930

VIRGINIA FORD . . . . Washington, D. C.
KATHRYN GLENN . . . . Norfolk, Va.
FRANCES GRIFFIN . . . . Norfolk, Va.
BETSY ROSS NICKOLSON . . . . Churchland, Va.
VIRGINIA PAUL . . . . Spring Lake, N. J.
LENORE SCHOFIELD . . . . Hampton, Va.
HARRIET SMITH . . . . Ashland, Va.
LUCY PILCHER . . . . Petersburg, Va.

Class of 1931

MARGARET FULLER . . . . Whiteville, N. C.
ELIZABETH GRIFFIN . . . . Norfolk, Va.
KATHERINE HASSELTINE . . . . Fortress Monroe, Va.
LOUISE PILCHER . . . . Petersburg, Va.
HELEN PORTER . . . . Virginia Beach, Va.
MARY LEWIS MAYHEW . . . . Roanoke, Va.
RUTH MILLER . . . . Dallas, Texas
DOROTHY REESE . . . . Norfolk, Va.

Pi Beta Phi is the oldest sorority and is second in the number of chapters in existence. It was founded at Monmouth College in 1861 and between that time and now has established chapters in 80 institutions. All but nine of these have lived.

The quarterly journal is called the Arrow.

PROGRESS NUMBER

PROGRESS NUMBER

Phi Mu

SORORES IN COLLEGIO

Class of 1928

GENE MILES . . . . Crisfield, Md.
EDNA SPITLER . . . . Luray, Va.
MARGARET SWEENEY . . . . Richmond, Va.
EDITH WILKINS . . . . San Antonio, Texas

Class of 1929

WYLLHART BAYLIS . . . . Columbia, S. C.
MARION BONNIWELL . . . . Harborton, Va.
NANCY BURKE . . . . Hampton, Va.
HELEN JOHNSON . . . . Franklin, Va.
RUTH JONES . . . . Franklin, Va.
MARION LANNING . . . . Pennington, N. J.

Class of 1930

SALLY BYRD FARMER . . . . Jetersville, Va.
ALICE HARWOOD . . . . Appomatox, Va.
EVELYN STEELE . . . . Tazewell, Va.
ELEANOR WILLIAMSON . . . . Vivian, W. Va.
GENEVIEVE WYATT . . . . White Sulphur Springs, W. Va.

Class of 1931

VIRGINIA BUSTON . . . . Tazewell, Va.
MARGARET JOERISSEN . . . . Freeport, Long Island
GENE KING . . . . Belle Haven, Va.
ELIZABETH SINCINDIVER . . . . Martinsburg, W. Va.
MARTHA SAVEDGE . . . . Franklin, Va.
DOROTHY SMITHER . . . . Newport News, Va.
BARBARA WYATT . . . . Hampton, Va.

Phi Mu was an outgrowth of a local society at Wesleyan College in 1852. In 1904 the name was changed to Phi Mu and expansion begun. At present there are 48 active and 7 inactive chapters on their rolls.

The quarterly Aglaia is the official publication.

PROGRESS NUMBER

173

PROGRESS NUMBER

Alpha Chi Omega

SORORES IN FACULTATE

KATHLEEN ALSOP   ALTHA HUNT

SORORES IN COLLEGIO

Class of 1928

NOMA FUQUA	Radford, Va.
PHYLLIS HUGHES	West Point, Va.
MARGARET HOWIE	Norfolk, Va.
CATHARINE CARTER	Richmond, Va.

Class of 1929

RUTH ANDREWS	Philadelphia, Penn.
RHODA FRY	Highland Springs, Va.
VIRGINIA HULL	Durbin, W. Va.
VIRGINIA MELTON	Fredricksburg, Va.
VIRGINIA GOULDMAN	Fredricksburg, Va.
MARY K. QUICK	Winchester, Va.
CAMILLA KELLAR	West Po!nt, Va.
MARY MORRISON	Albion, Mich.
CATHERINE REYNOLDS	Danville, Va.

Class of 1930

MARTHA GRESHAM	Newport News, Va.
LELIA JACKSON	Atlanta, Ga.
DEETTE JONES	Atlanta, Ga.
MARGARET JOHNSON	Norfolk, Va.
MERILLA HICKS	Granville, N. Y.
GENE ROUNTREE	Suffolk, Va.
VERNETTE BEEBE	Norfolk, Va.

Class of 1931

ELENOR SMITH	Washington, D. C.
ELIZABETH ALLEN	King and Queen, Va.
ISABEL GOUGH	Baltimore, Md.

Alpha Chi Omega was founded at De Pauw University in 1885. The chapter roll includes 47 active chapters with no inactive ones.

The Lyre is the official organ and appears four times each session.

PROGRESS NUMBER

PROGRESS NUMBER

Delta Chi Delta

Class of 1928

MARTHA CLAIBORNE	Ashland, Va.
MARTHA L. HALE	Elk Creek, Va.
ROSE M. FLANNERY	Portsmouth, Va.
ELIZABETH NICHOLAS	Dayton, Ohio
GEORGIA SHERRY	Richmond, Va.

Class of 1929

INEZ BAKER	Cartersville, Va.
FRANCES M. FORD	Cartersville, Va.
FRANCE LORD	Newport News, Va.
MARY MATHEW	Portsmouth, Va.
VIRGINIA NICHOLAS	Dayton, Ohio
MARY G. RIDEOUT	Roanoke, Va.

Class of 1930

MARION HARRISON	Richmond, Va.
ELIZABETH HUFF	Norfolk, Va.
ESTHER REEVE	Philadelphia, Penn.

Class of 1931

MARGARET ELLIS	Ashland, Va.
BLANCHE WOOD PIERCE	Windsor, N. C.

Delta Chi Delta is a local sorority organized at
William and Mary in 1927.

PROGRESS NUMBER

PROGRESS NUMBER

Chi Alpha

Class of 1928

ETTA CLEMENTS . . . . Lee Hall, Va.
NAOMI CLEMENTS . . . . Lee Hall, Va.
KATHERINE FITZSIMMONS . . . . Zelienope, Penn.
ANNIE BOZARTH . . . . Williamsburg, Va.
KATHERINE TOPPING . . . . Newport News, Va.

Class of 1929

AGNES BRITTINGHAM . . . . Wachaprague, Va.
MILDRED MAITLAND . . . . Era, Va.
MURIEL JOHNSON . . . . White Plains, N. Y.
GENEVIEVE HOFFMAN . . . . White Plains, N. Y.
SARAH PENN . . . . Roanoke, Va.
HELEN H. OSMOND . . . . Berkley Springs, W. Va.

Class of 1930

GRACE BALLARD . . . . Exmore, Va.
LUCY MAE BOSWELL . . . . Petersburg, Va.
ELIZABETH LANIER . . . . Petersburg, Va.

Class of 1931

MARY EDGAR . . . . Richmond, Va.
EVELYN HAINES . . . . Chester, Va.
MARIAN MULLEN . . . . Adena, Ohio
KATHERINE COTHRAN . . . . Lockport, N. Y.
CAROLYN WHITE . . . . Scottsville, Va.
CELESTE WINN . . . . Victoria, Va.
AGNESS WINN . . . . Victoria, Va.
ALMA WATKINSON . . . . Greenbrush, Va.
EDITH RICHARDSON . . . . Portsmouth, Va.
IRMA ADAMS . . . . Formosa, Va.
MARGARET DIFFEN . . . . New York City

Chi Alpha is a local sorority organized at William
and Mary in 1927.

PROGRESS NUMBER

179

Pan-Hellenic Council

Kappa Alpha Theta

LOIS WILSON
VIRGINIA FLOYD

Phi Mu

NANCY BURKE
HELEN JOHNSON

Pi Beta Phi

MARJORIE LACY
POLLY HINES

Kappa Kappa Gamma

MARGARET VENABLE
FRANCES THOMSON

Delta Chi Delta

MARY G. RIDEOUT
GEORGIA SHERRY

Chi Alpha

SARAH PENN
KATHERINE TOPPING

Chi Omega

LAURA WHITEHEAD
FLORENCE SAUNDERS

Alpha Chi Omega

KATHERINE CARTER
NOMA FUQUA

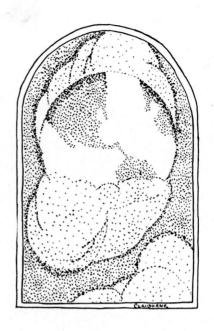

Clubs and
Honorary Fraternities

The F. H. C. Society

(The Flat Hat Club)

MEMBERS

DR. W. A. HAMILTON	ALAN COOK
DR. L. C. LINDSLEY	WILLIAM LINN
DR. R. C. YOUNG	WILLIAM WEST
DR. W. A. MONTGOMERY	DONALD VAN WORMER
HERBERT GANTER	NATHAN CAFFEE
GEORGE REILLY	JAMES ROBERTSON
JOHN TODD	WARFIELD WINN
JOSEPH CHANDLER	KENNETH BEATTY
JOHN BENTLEY	LAWRENCE I'ANSON

The Flat Hat Club is the oldest living college organization in America, having been founded at the College of William and Mary on November 11, 1750, thus antedating the Phi Beta Kappa Society by twenty-six years. On its rolls may be found the names of Jefferson and others of the college's famous alumni, including the long list of notables in the Spotswood Club of Old Virginia.

In spite of all efforts to attract the Society into other colleges, it has consistently maintained a policy which is opposed to expansion, preferring to remain local and retain its tradition.

PROGRESS NUMBER

183

PROGRESS NUMBER

Omicron Delta Kappa

MEMBERS

Dr. J. A. C. Chandler	Herbert Ganter	E. Carlton Macon
Dr. R. L. Morton	Arthur Matsu	W. G. Thompson
Dr. J. D. Carter	M. C. Davis	James Robertson
Dr. W. A. Hamilton	A. K. Turner	M. Weldon Thompson
Dr. J. R. Geiger	D. K. Van Wormer	Upton B. Thomas
Dr. E. G. Swem	J. A. Cook	John B. Green
Dr. D. W. Davis	H. Chris Somers	W. N. James
Dr. W. T. Hodges	K. B. Beatty	F. O. Clarke
Mr. A. G. Williams	J. M. Eason	T. G. Burke
J. Wilder Tasker	W. H. Elliott	E. P. Simpkins
John Todd	L. W. I'Anson	N. M. Caffee
George Reilly	E. T. Justis	W. B. Bolton
	W. M. Linn	

Omicron Delta Kappa was founded at Washington and Lee University in December, 1914. The Eta Circle was established at the College of William and Mary in 1921. It recognizes eminence in all forms of college activities and has for its purpose the bringing together of the campus leaders for the general good of the institution in one body.

It is recognized as one of the highest honors that can be given an undergraduate student, because of the ideals and standards which it holds.

185

PROGRESS NUMBER

Sigma Upsilon

GORDON HOPE CHAPTER
Established 1914

FRATRES IN FACULTATE

Dr. J. Lesslie Hall	Dr. W. A. Hamilton	Mr. G. H. Gelsinger
Dr. W. A. Montgomery	Dr. J. R. Geiger	Mr. Glenwood Clark

FRATRES IN COLLEGIO

Willard N. James	George W. Reilly	J. J. Van Putten
D. K. Van Wormer	Marion Nolley	Edward Fales
Nathan M. Caffee	John B. Green	William Vincent
Herbert L. Ganter	Robert Barrett	Norman Patterson
	Boyd Carter	

Sigma Upsilon, an honorary literary fraternity, was founded in 1906 by the union of four local literary groups in various southern colleges. It grants membership primarily on ability and interest in literature and usually elects twice a year from the members of the three upper classes.

Sigma Upsilon was the third honorary fraternity on the campus of William and Mary, having been organized here in 1914. It was preceded by the F. H. C. Society and by Phi Beta Kappa.

PROGRESS NUMBER

Phi Delta Gamma

MEMBERS

DR. W. A. HAMILTON	M. WELDON THOMPSON	D. ARTHUR KELSEY
DR. K. J. HOKE	ROBERT S. BARRETT	WILLIAM H. ELLIOTT
DR. J. G. POLLARD	TRUMAN WELLING	A. P. HENDERSON
DR. W. A. R. GOODWIN	NATHAN M. CAFFEE	WILLARD N. JAMES
DR. R. L. MORTON	A. EARLE GARRETT	EDWIN LAMBERTH
DR. G. W. SPICER	LAWRENCE N. MORSCHER	RANDOLPH VAIDEN
PROF H. C. KREBS	GORDON E. CAMPBELL	R. R. JONES
GEORGE W. REILLY	C. H. RUSSELL	W. B. BOLTON
H. CHRIS SOMERS	EDWARD H. HILL	SAMUEL G. STAPLES
	CHARLES M. HAILEY	

The professional forensic fraternity of Phi Delta Gamma was founded in 1924 to foster interest in literary work, debating, and dramaturgy. This, William and Mary Chapter, was one of the original chapters and has steadily grown in influence on this campus by stimulating intersociety rather than intercollegiate forensics since its founding.

It invites inquiry on and constructive criticism of all branches of forensics through its official organ, "The Literary Scroll."

187

Alpha Kappa Psi

OMEGA CHAPTER

MEMBERS

Dr. W. A. Hamilton	Joseph James	James Kelley
Prof. Gibbs	C. Hayden Russell	Dave Moore
M. C. Stribling	Arthur Matsu	Arthur Nolde
W. G. Thompson	James Addington	A. D. Yeary
George Mapp	F. A. Gessford	W. J. Blackwell
Joe Hornbarger	Robert Beeler	Lowell Ayers
James Robertson	E. Carlton Macon	Terry Crossfield
E. Armstrong Smith	Garland Johnson	J. H. Diebert

Alpha Kappa Psi is a professional commercial fraternity that limits its membership to students who are seeking a degree in business. It was the first national fraternity of its kind and was the first to admit students of evening college classes.

The Omega Chapter was founded here in 1921 and has kept pace with the growth of the School of Business Administration, until it has become one of the strongest honorary organizations on the campus.

COLONIAL ECHO

Pi Gamma Mu

Founded 1924; Virginia Alpha established 1924

Members

Kathleen Alsop	Joseph E. Rowe
J. A. C. Chandler	Elizabeth Schmucker
Joseph R. Geiger	Earl G. Swem
M. G. H. Gelsinger	John B. Todd
W. A. R. Goodwin	Paul A. Warren
George E. Gregory	Roscoe Conklin Young
Channing M. Hall	Herbert L. Ganter
Emily M. Hall	William J. Hogan
John Lesslie Hall	Elizabeth Saunders
William A. Hamilton	Lucille Foster
William T. Hodges	E. P. Simpkins
Kremer J. Hoke	Elizabeth Gordon
David J. King	Norma Doran
George W. Reilly	Wayne F. Gibbs

Pi Gamma Mu is a social science honor society which was founded December 1, 1924, for the purpose of securing co-operation in the study of social problems.

Virginia Alpha Chapter has been on the campus since the year of its founding. It is open only to members of the graduating class, from which candidates are picked by the various department heads.

Chi Beta Phi

BETA CHAPTER
Established 1921

HONORARY MEMBERS

Dr. D. W. Davis
Dr. W. A. Hamilton
Dr. R. G. Robb
Dr. W. G. Guy
Dr. P. A. Warren

Dr. J. E. Rowe
Dr. R. C. Young
Dr. A. W. Dearing
R. A. Winborne
J. G. Jantz
Maj. O. De Carre

Capt. T. P. Walsh
Capt. H. R. Behrene
Capt. Arnesorum
Capt. D. W. Cleary
Lieut. Arthur Lavery

ACTIVE MEMBERS

R. G. Todd
A. K. Turner
Logan Hudson
H. C. Somers
Manley Mallard
Conrad Pierce

George F. Wilkins
M. Weldon Thompson
Nathan M. Caffee
Archer D. Farmer
Walter A. Porter
Edward T. Justis

Henry Crigler

Chi Beta Phi is a national scientific fraternity founded in 1916, at Randolph-Macon College. Its purpose is the promotion of interests in the sciences. To be eligible for membership one must have shown a marked interest in science.

PROGRESS NUMBER

Theta Chi Delta

ALPHA THETA CHAPTER

HONORARY

Dr. R. G. Robb   Dr. A. W. Dearing

Dr. W. G. Guy   Dr. W. A. Hamilton

Capt. Thomas P. Walsh

ACTIVE

H. M. Bland	J. B. Hozier	W. A. Porter
Thomas H. Christie	E. T. Justis	H. C. Smith
F. S. Finch	Henry Keister	Hugh O. Staley
Jack Grizzard	Manley Mallard	R. G. Todd
James Harrison	William Melvin	A. K. Turner
Edward Hill		Warfield Winn

Theta Chi Delta, honorary chemical fraternity, was founded in 1921 at Lombard College. Membership comes as a reward for high scholarship and unusual merit in the department of chemistry.

The Alpha Theta Chapter, at the College of William and Mary, has in the past given an annual chemical exhibit to which the whole student body is invited. This chapter has been very active in aiding the department of chemistry.

PROGRESS NUMBER

Kappa Phi Kappa

OMICRON CHAPTER

Dr. W. A. Hamilton	S. N. Brown	James Gaskins, Jr.
Dr. J. A. Chandler	R. N. Gladding	S. A. Ozlin
Dr. W. T. Hodges	E. P. Simpkins, Jr.	B. D. Pattie
W. G. Neal	M. W. Thompson	C. H. Russell
H. C. Somers	Mr. H. C. Krebs	J. L. A. Motley
G. M. Nolley	Mr. C. M. Faithful	W. A. Porter
J. L. Hudson	Mr. John Boyton Todd	W. B. Atkisson
W. B. Bolton	Henry Ball	R. R. Poole

As a result of the remarkable growth of the Department of Education here, Kappa Phi Kappa established a chapter at the College in 1925. The fraternity is a national professional educational society, which is open to all white male students who are taking, or have taken, courses in the Department of Education. Membership is not limited to undergraduate students, but is attainable by both graduates and faculty members.

The chapter here on the campus is recognized as one of the best organizations here.

Sigma Pi Sigma

Honorary Physics Fraternity

SIGMA ZETA CHAPTER

HONORARY MEMBERS

CAPT. HENRY R. BEHRENS	DR. W. A. HAMILTON	CAPT. THOMAS P. WALSH
LIEUT. EDWARD C. COWEN	DR. W. A. MERRYMON	DR. R. C. YOUNG

ACTIVE MEMBERS

WM. B. ATKISSON	T. B. HALL	J. L. JOHNSON
NATHAN M. CAFFEE	A. M. HENLEY	EDWARD T. JUSTIS
HENRY CRIGLER	JOHN B. HOZIER	STANLEY POWELL
RAYMOND DRISCOLL	LOGAN HUDSON	J. R. JONES

Sigma Pi Sigma has not yet been on the campus a year as a national organization, having existed prior to June, 1927, as the Phi Delta, local honorary physics fraternity. Sigma Pi Sigma has the distinction of being the only national physics fraternity in the country. In spite of its extreme youth it is already proving itself a virile and healthy organization.

Eligibility rules require a student to be taking an advanced course in physics and to be making a grade that is above the average. This group of men has always been interested in the Department of Physics here and co-operates with it on all occasions.

193

Beta Alpha Psi

KAPPA CHAPTER

HONORARY MEMBERS

DR. W. A. HAMILTON   WAYNE F. GIBBS
C. A. FRYXELL

STUDENT MEMBERS

W. G. THOMPSON   W. J. BLACKWELL
GEORGE T. MORECOCK

Beta Alpha Psi, organized at the University of Illinois in February, 1919, is a national professional accounting fraternity, which has as its purpose the fostering of the ideal of service in accountancy, the acting as a medium between professional men, instructors, students, and any others who are interested in accounting, the encouraging of high moral, scholastic, and professional standards in its members, and the developing of cordial intercourse among its members and the members of the profession. It is only open to students who are taking accounting with a view of making it their profession.

194

Alpha Club

FRANCES GORDON   PAGE DRINKER
MARJORIE LACY   RUTH JAMES
ELIZABETH LAM   BILLIE SHELTON

HONORARY MEMBERS

DR. GRACE LANDRUM   MISS HELEN F. WEEKS

The Alpha Club was established at William and Mary several years ago to serve as a medium through which the leaders of the girls' student body might discuss the problems confronting them. It recognizes pre-eminence in the various fields of campus activity and brings the leaders into close touch with each other. Membership is restricted to seniors and is the highest undergraduate honor that a woman can obtain.

Edith Baer Club

FACULTY MEMBERS

MISS LEONE REAVES   MISS LILLIAN CUMMINGS

MISS MARTHA HOLLIDAY   MRS. H. M. STRYKER

OFFICERS

KATHERINE RHODES . . . . *President*

KATHERINE WATSON . . . . *Vice-President*

ALICE CRUTCHFIELD . . . . *Secretary*

MADOLINE WATSON . . . . *Treasurer*

PHYLLIS HUGHES . . *Chairman of Program Committee*

ELIZA HUNTER . . . . *Chairman of Ways and Means*

MEMBERS

DOROTHY CHALKLEY	ELNA SPITLER
PAULINE COGLE	WILLOW SATTERFIELD
ALICE CRUTCHFIELD	CHRISTINE LAUTZ
PAGE DRINKER	KATHERINE WATSON
DOROTHY FARRAR	MADOLINE WATSON
PHYLLIS HUGHES	ELIZA HUNTER
GRACE MILLER	ELIZABETH DUKE
MARGARET MURRAY	MILDRED DUDLEY
JULIA SANDERS	KATHERINE RHODES

The Edith Baer Club, founded in honor of a former professor here, devotes its time to the study of home economics and related subjects. With a well-defined program the Club, by means of lectures and study programs, furthers the science of home economics in a systematic and intelligent way.

PROGRESS NUMBER

197

Chi Delta Phi

WILLIAM AND MARY CHAPTER

MARJORIE LACY   CONSTANCE JAMIESON
HARRIETTE SMITH   EDITH DODD
HANNAH MARGOLIS   FRANCES LEWIS
DE ETTE JONES   PEGGY NININGER

EDITH RICHARDSON

Chi Delta Phi was founded at the University of Tennessee in 1919 and the Theta Chapter was established here in 1922. Its purpose is to form a body of women, who by their interest in literature and by their influence will uphold the highest ideals of a liberal education. It corresponds to the Sigma Upsilon literary fraternity in its purpose and ideals, its founding having been agitated by a former national secretary of the Sigma Upsilon fraternity.

PROGRESS NUMBER

Sigma Delta Psi

E. C. Mason   Y. O. Kent

E. T. Justis   M. C. Davis

A. A. Matsu

Sigma Delta Psi, established at the University of Indiana in 1912, has as its object the encouragement of moral, physical and mental development among college students. To become eligible a student must meet certain standards in different events that make its membership a coveted prize.

199

PROGRESS NUMBER

Los Quixotescos

FACULTY

Dr. E. C. BRANCHI   Dr. E. G. SWEM

Dr. A. G. WILLIAMS

ACTIVE MEMBERS

ISABEL BRUGADA . . . . *President*

KITTY TOPPING . . . . *Secretary*

GERALD CALLIS . . . . *Treasurer*

ELEANOR CALKINS	FRANK GLENN
GERALD CALLIS	MARGARET HALL
LOIS EVANS	VIRGINIA HARPER
NORRIS HALPERN	DeETTE JONES
WILLIAM HALPERN	CARLTON MACON
JOSEPH HANCOCK	HELEN MOFFETT
PAULINE HINES	RUTH MILLER
MARGARET HOWIE	WILLIAM MUNSEY
ALICE KERR	H. A. NEWLAND
PHYLLIS LOGAN	ELIZABETH NICHOLAS
MAY REILLY	LOUISE PILCHER
LOUIS ROTGIN	LUCY PILCHER
MARY THOMAS	META RICHARDSON
KITTY TOPPING	ELIZABETH SAUNDERS
CHARLES ARMENTROUT	JAMES SAVAGE
LUCY BOSWELL	CHARLES SCAMMON
DOROTHY BUNDY	CONNIE SHEREN
ANNE COCIAPPA	AL TURNER
SUSAN CARPENTER	ELIZABETH VAIDEN
ALLAN COOK	ELEANOR VAUGHN
CATHERINE COTHRAN	ALENE WALKER
VIRGINIA FORD	EMMA WARING
RANDOLPH GLADDING	

PROGRESS NUMBER

201

PROGRESS NUMBER

The Wythe Law Club

Founded in 1921.

H. C. Somers . . . . *Chancellor*
R. C. Power . . . . *Vice-Chancellor*
George Moriarty . . . . *Clerk*
F. O. Clarke . . . . *Bailiff*
Dr. W. A. Hamilton . . . *Faculty Adviser*

Members

Dr. W. W. Woodbridge	Dr. G. W. Spicer
Dr. J. A. C. Chandler	Dr. J. R. Geiger
Dr. J. G. Pollard	Mr. G. W. Reilly
L. M. Ober	J. L. Lewis
C. H. Russell	M. B. Swetz
G. C. Campbell	L. B. Maxey
H. Schey	

PROGRESS NUMBER

The Clayton-Grimes Biology Club

HONORARY MEMBERS

MRS. D. W. DAVIS   MRS. A. F. DOLLOFF   MRS. P. A. WARREN

OFFICERS

First Term		*Second Term*	
W. A. PORTER	*President*	W. A. PORTER	*President*
GEORGIA SHERRY	*Vice-President*	MARGARET BILISOLY	*Vice-President*
HANNAH MARGOLIS	*Secretary*	HANNAH MARGOLIS	*Secretary*
LAWRENCE MORSCHER	*Treasurer*	LAWRENCE MORSCHER	*Treasurer*

ARNOLD MOTLEY, *Chairman of Program Committee*

MARGARET BILISOLY, *Chairman of Refreshment Committee*

MARGARET BILISOLY	MARY E. JOHNSTON	BERNARD RABINOWITZ
MARGRETA BLUME	NANCY JOHNSTON	ESTER REEVE
THOMAS H. CHRISTIE	ROY JOHNSON	H. M. SANGER
C. E. CLEVENGER	KATHERINE KAHLE	DORIS RATHEIN
G. C. COX	GEORGE LAMPROS	GEORGIA SHERRY
MARTHA CLAIBORNE	HANNAH MARGOLIS	H. C. SMITH
MAX CHARNICK	LAWRENCE MORSCHER	HUGH STALEY
DR. D. W. DAVIS	ARNOLD MOTLEY	GEORGE SCHMUTZ
FRANCIS GORDON	ROSE MOUNTCASTLE	ZELDA SWARTZ
RANDOLPH GLADDING	GLADYS OMOHUNDRO	JOHN TURLEY
C. E. GLENN	W. A. PORTER	ROBERT TERRELL
E. H. HILL	L. N. PRINCE	GEORGE WATTS
C. P. JONES		DR. P. A. WARREN

Delta Mu Chi

Founded in 1926

Gessford, Floyd	Caffee, N. M.
Morecock, G. T.	Harley, C. M.
Mallard, Manley	Stribling, Mit
Ober, L. M.	O'Brien, Warren
Thompson, M. W.	Ayers, J. G.
Price, Robert	

Delta Mu Chi is a social organization on the campus whose purpose is the strengthening of the bonds existing between those students who are already members of the Order of DeMolay. Membership has no class distinction and no requirements other than membership in the DeMolays.

PROGRESS NUMBER

Eta Sigma Phi

Classical Fraternity

OFFICERS

ELIZABETH SAUNDERS . . . . *President*
ALICE KERR . . . . *Secretary*
E. P. SIMPKINS . . . . *Treasurer*
GLADYS CAULKINS, *Faculty Member*

MEMBERS

DORIS RATHEIN	MILDA COHEN	MARIAM SILBERGER
LOUISE RICE	ELIZA GEORGE	SAM WILCOX
MARY FLEET	MELBA GRAVELY	NANCY WARD
BILLIE SHELTON	EDITH HOLLOWELL	FRANCES FORD
ETTA CLEMENTS	SARAH HUGHES	JEANETTE WARD
	KATHERINE TOPPING	

ASSOCIATE MEMBERS

DR. W. A. MONTGOMERY   DR. M. G. A. GELSINGER
DR. E. G. SWEM   MR. A. G. WILLIAMS

PROGRESS NUMBER

Kappa Delta Pi

Founded at University of Illinois, 1911

National Honorary Educational Fraternity

FACULTY

Dr. J. A. C. Chandler   Miss Helen Weeks
Dr. W. T. Hodges   Miss Martha Barksdale

ACTIVE MEMBERS

May Reilly	Frances Lord	Doris Rathiene
Norma Doran	Hayden Gwalthney	Henry Crigler
Thelma Stinnett	Frances Ford	William Bolton
Elizabeth Saunders	Melba Gravely	Raymond Driscall
Alene Walker	Mary Land	Henry Ball
Louise Rice	Lucile Foster	Harold Newland
Mildred Liebrecht	Eulah Massey	Weldon Thompson
	Catherine Carter	
	Margaret Howie	

Kappa Delta Pi is an honorary educational fraternity for juniors and seniors who have a grade above the average and have completed some work in education. Its distinguishing feature is that it has a Laureate Chapter composed of leading educators throughout the country. On this campus it forms an interested professional group in one of the largest departments of the College.

Art Club

Virginia Floyd . . . . . . *President*		Henry Ball . . . . *Treasurer*
Elsie West . . . . . . *Vice-President*		Mary Wall Christian . . . . *Secretary*

Kitty Harveycutter	Eleanor Ford	Betsy Nicholson
Catherine Randolph	Mrs. L. W. Lane	Miss Mary Irwin
Elizabeth Duke	Dr. Landrum	Gertrude Henderson
Armada Clark	Emma Waring	Margaret Diffin
Mrs. R. L. Morton	Dorothy Boone	Katherine Cone
Jane Worthington	Henry Ball	Mary Bullock
Mrs. Guy	Katherine Topping	Anna Henderson
Dr. Guy	Lois Wilson	Mrs. Goodwin
Mrs. K. J. Hoke	Rebecca Ball	Bula Smith
Elizabeth Ambler	Ernestine Penn	Miss Weeks
Mary Ribble	Elizabeth Sexton	Mrs. Krebs
Mrs. E. G. Swem	Betty St. Clair	Dorothy Davie
Dr. Goodwin	Jane St. Clair	Katherine Nicholas
Miss Hayes	Miss Cummings	Anne Fiddler
Miss Goodwin	Grace Ballard	Betty Duval
Margaret Morris	Evelyn Wayne	Etta Clements
Miss Johnson	Hannah Margolis	Naomi Clements
Miss Sellevold	Miss Hunt	George Schmutz
Lois Evans	Florence Schofield	Miss L. Irwin
Anne Bozarth	Morrice Vaccarrelli	Estelle Lance
Margaret Murray	Dorothy Maier	Viola Barrett
	Alma Mae Clark	

Gibbons Club

COLLEGE OF WILLIAM AND MARY

WILLIAM G. THOMPSON, JR. . . . . *President*
HELEN LORENZEN . . . . *Vice-President*
CHARLES MARCIANO . . . . *Secretary-Treasurer*

MEMBERS

RALPH FERRANDINI	RALPH DEFALCO	WILLIAM SCOTT
ARCHER MAHONEY	PAUL BALDACCI	LUCILLE CALURA
WM. F. O'NEILL	FRED CASSIDY	MARGARET KERR
H. J. RABBEN	MITCHELL MOZELESKI	MARGARET DIGGS
ANNE CACIOPPO	RAYMOND DORAN	NORMA DORAN
OLGA SKORA	FRANCIS S. THOMPSON	VIRGINIA PAUL
SARAH HUGHES	JAMES MURPHEY	GEORGE MORIARITY
MARGARET SWEENEY	ANTHONY COSTANTINO	FRED FINCH
MARY MENTZEN	ANDREW J. COPPOLA	FRANK GRAVEN
MARION MULLEN	WALTER DEMARTINI	HERBERT GANTER
STEPHEN CASSAGRANDE	ANDREW R. COPPOLA	H. G. PARKER
GERARD FARENOLA	DORMINICK MELFI	WILLIAM FIELDS

FACULTY

PROF. E. C. BRANCHI   PROF. H. J. AMIEL
PROF. GEORGE E. BROOKS   MISS ISABEL BRUGADA

RESIDENT MEMBERS

MRS. TUCKER JONES   ALICE REINECKE
VIRGINIA JONES   MRS. BULIFANT
MR. AND MRS. REINECKE   MR. AND MRS. MACKEY

PROGRESS NUMBER

H₂E Club

Health—Happiness—Efficiency

OFFICERS

ALICE CHEWNING . . . . *President*
HARRIETTE ZIMMERMAN . . . . *Treasurer*
HELEN H. OSMOND . . . . *Secretary*

MEMBERS

ALICE CHEWNING	HELEN OSMOND
MARY QUICK	HARRIETTE ZIMMERMAN
ELIZEBETH TANNER	NANCY BURKE
GENE MILES	LENA DESHAZO

PAGE VAUGHAN

HONORARY MEMBERS

MARTHA BARKSDALE MARGUERITE WYNNE-ROBERTS
L. TUCKER JONES

The H₂E Club is a physical education society for women. It has chosen a name that is self-explanatory. It encourages health, happiness and efficiency in its members, through the study of Physical Education.

PROGRESS NUMBER

G. G. G. Club

POLLY HINES, *President*

EVA ATKINSON
ELIZABETH AMBLER
ELSIE BEEBE
HELEN BRISTOW
MARGARET BAILEY
FRANCES BURGWYN
LUCILLE BURKE
SUSAN CARPENTER
DOT CHALKLEY
BETTY ST. CLAIR
JANE ST. CLAIR
MARION CHEYNE
CLARICE COOK
ELIZABETH DUKE
SARA ANNE EVERETT
DOT FARRAR
MELBA GRAVELY
ELIZABETH GRIFFIN
ANNE FIDDLER
MARGARET FULLER
MARGARET HALL

CLARE HARGROVE
CATHERINE HUNTER
MABEL IRWIN
RUTH JAMES
CONSTANCE JAMIESON
MARGARET JOERRISON
GENE KING
NAN LANGHORNE
MARJORIE LACEY
PHYLLIS LOGAN
ANN TENSEY
HILDA MILLER
GRACE MILLER
RUTH MILLER
BETSY NICHOLSON
LUCY PILCHER
LOUISE PILCHER
VIRGINIA PAUL
LUCILLE PARKER
BETSY PRICE

MARY RIBBLE
DOROTHY REISE
MARY RUSH
CHARLOTTE SANFORD
BILLIE SHELTON
ELIZABETH SMITH
HARRIETT SMITH
FRANCES SAUNDERS
HAZEL SAUNDERS
ELIZABETH SEXTON
LOIS STONE
MARGARET SWEENEY
VIRGINIA TURMAN
ANNE TRENTE
ELIZABETH TROUT
MARY TROUT
SUSANNE WHEELER
LAURA WHITEHEAD
TIXIE WIMBISH
JANE WORTHINGTON
FRANCIS SHEPHERD

PROGRESS NUMBER

K. O. B. Club

VIRGINIA FLOYD, *President*

VIRGINIA ARMISTEAD
VIRGINIA ALEXANDER
BECKY BALL
VIOLA BARRET
DOT BROUGHTON
DORIS CLARKE
EDITH DODD
ELIZABETH DUKE
VIRGINIA FORD
VIRGINIA FARENHOLT
KITTY HARVEYCUTTER
VIRGINIA HARPER

HELEN PORTER
HALL, IRMA
DOROTHY HALLEGAN
MARION HANDY
MARION HARRISON
ALICE HOLMES
LOUISE JAMES
RUTH JAMES
CHRIS LANTZ
ESTHER LOWE
MARY LEWIS MAYHEW
ELIZABETH MOORE
PEGGY NININGER

ERNESTINE RENN
KATHERINE RHOADS
DOROTHY RHOADS
JUDY SANDERS
VIRGINIA SMITH
DOT SMITHERS
FRANCES THOMPSON
ALICE VEQUBART
POLLY VENABLE
PAGE VAUGHAN
ELIZABETH VAIDEN
LOIS WILSON

CROSSFIELD
Vice-President

WEST
President

BURKE
Secretary-Treasurer

Cotillion Club

L. C. AYRES
JOHN G. AYRES
L. M. ANDERSON
J. F. BARNES
WILLIAM BOZARTH
J. M. BRIDGEFORTH
WM. B. BOLTON
KENNETH BEATTY
TERRY CROSSFIELD
JOHN CLEMENS
WALTER COLEMAN
ALBERT E. COX
F. O. CLARK
ROY CHARLES
IRWIN DAVIS
H. T. DAVIS
J. J. DAVIES
R. E. DOYLE
JULIAN ETHERIDGE
JOHN B. GREEN
EDGAR GARRARD
CLARENCE GARRARD
HERBERT GANTER
J. W. HURT

F. L. HAYMAN
E. K. HOWARD
CHARLES HAILEY
VERNON HAYMAN
L. I'ANSON
NORMAN JOHNSON
JONES
W. N. JAMES
Y. O. KENT
EDWARD LEACH
B. F. LYNCH
G. H. MAPP
D. S. MOORE
MacMILLAN
RICHARD MULLONEY
ART MATSU
VANCE MacDONOUGH
J. A. NOLDE
RUDOLPH NOLDE
W. G. NEALE
M. T. O'FERRALL
NED OWENS
SHELTON PETERS
FRED PERSON
GEORGE PORTER

BOB PULLEY
BARTON PATTIE
LEWIS RUEGER
J. M. ROBERTSON
CLARENCE RIVES
ROBERTS
A. R. SIMMONS
GEORGE SYER
EARLE SWEM
SEWELL SIMPSON
E. P. SIMPKINS
A. K. TURNER
L. R. TAYLOR
W. G. THOMPSON
FRANCIS THOMPSON
J. B. THOMAS
UPTON THOMAS
THOMAS VARNEY
W. P. VINEYARD
RANDOLPH VAIDEN
W. C. WEST
GEORGE WILKINS
MILTON G. WHITE
W. W. WAIN

PROGRESS NUMBER

LAURA WHITEHEAD
Vice-President

ELIZABETH DUKE
President

FRANCES THOMSON
Secretary-Treasurer

German Club

MEMBERS

VIRGINIA ARMISTEAD	MARY DUNLOP	MARGARET JOHNSON	J. ELIZABETH SMITH
VIRGINIA ALEXANDER	LORNA DENNISON	CHRISTINE LANTZ	FRANCES SAUNDERS
DOROTHY BROUGHTON	MARGARET DIFFIN	MILDRED LIEBRECHT	ELIZABETH SEXTON
DOROTHY BOONE	LOIS EVANS	PHYLLIS LOGAN	FRANCES SHEPHERD
NANCY BURKE	SARA ANNA EVERETT	MARION LANNING	HARRIETT SMITH
THELMA BRYANT	MARGARET ELLIS	LOIS LACY	MARGARET SWEENEY
MARGARET BAILEY	ANNE FIDLER	DOROTHY LANKFORD	EVELYN STEELE
REBECCA BALL	VIRGINIA FLOYD	FRANCES LEWIS	MARION SARGENT
ELSIE BEEBE	NOMA FUQUA	ESTER LOWE	LENORE SCHOFIELD
LUCY MAE BOSWELL	DOROTHY FARRAR	ETHEL LITTLE	LOIS STONE
LUCILLE BURKE	VIRGINIA FARINHOLT	GRACE MILLER	JULIA SANDERS
BILLY BAYLISS	VIRGINIA FORD	MARY MOTLEY	DOROTHY SMITHERS
VIOLA BARRETT	MARGARET FULLER	LUCY MILLER	ELIZABETH SINCINDIVER
VIRGINIA BUXSTON	SALLY BYRD FARMER	RUTH MILLER	FRANCES THOMSON
HELEN BRISTOW	MELBA GRAVELY	HILDA MILLER	VIRGINIA TURMAN
MARION BONNIWELL	KATHERINE GLENN	ANNE ELIZABETH MOORE	DOROTHY TRAVILIAN
MARTHA CLAIBORNE	MARTHA GRESHAM	MARY NININGER	MARY GRACE TROUT
DORRIS CLARKE	ELIZABETH GRIFFIN	BETSY ROSS NICHOLSON	ANNE TRENT
DOROTHY CHALKLEY	POLLY HINES	VIRGINIA NELSON	ELIZABETH TROUT
SUSAN CARPENTER	VIRGINIA HARPER	VIRGINIA PAUL	EMILY VAN LEAR
KATHLEEN CONE	ELIZA HUNTER	LUCY PILCHER	ALICE URQUHART
SUE CORNICK	KITTY HARVEYCUTTER	CONSTANCE PAGE	PAGE VAUGHAN
ALICE CHEWNING	DOROTHY HALLIGAN	CATHERINE PENDLETON	POLLY VENABLE
KATHERINE COOK	IRMA HALL	ELIZABETH PRICE	ELIZABETH VAIDEN
VIRGINIA CRAWFORD	MARJORIE HARRIS	HELEN PORTER	LOIS WILSON
CLARICE COOK	MARION HARRISON	LOUISE PILCHER	LAURA WHITEHEAD
RUTH CULTRA	HELEN HOSTETTLER	BETSY PRICE	MADOLIN WALTON
KATHERINE CARTER	CATHERINE HUNTER	MARY QUICK	GENEVIVE WYATT
MARION CHEYNE	MARION HANDY	KATHERINE RHODES	EDITH WILKINS
ELIZABETH DUKE	CLAIRE HARGROVE	MARY G. RIDEOUT	JANE WORTHINGTON
EDTIH DODD	CONSTANCE JAMISON	EDITH RICHARDSON	BARBARA WYATT
FLORENCE DABNEY	RUTH JONES	MARY ROBERTSON	SHIRLEY WRIGHT
ELIZABETH DUNLOP	LOUISE JAMES	DOROTHY REESE	

PROGRESS NUMBER

The "7" Society

John Buxton Todd, '25
George Washintgon Reilly, '26
Arthur Matsu, '27

Class of 1928

William C. West . . . . *President*
Kenneth B. Beatty . . . . *Vice-President*
Melvin C. Davis . . . . *Secretary*

J. Alan Cook   William Collier Linn
Lawrence Warren I'Anson   Edward Carlton Macon

214

PROGRESS NUMBER

"13" Club

FRATRES IN URBE

BOB WALLACE   BILL HENLEY

FRATRES IN COLLEGIO

JESSIE MILES   JIMMIE ROBERTSON
ART MATSU   DUTCH ROBERTS
YEL KENT   GEORGE WILKINS
PAT PATTERSON   TOM BURKE
MEB DAVIS   F. O. CLARK

JEW REUGER

GOATS

TOM VARNEY   ED JUSTIS

215

History Club

Founded 1924.

Dr. R. L. Morton	Shelton Peters
Dr. Kathleen Bruce	Carol Brooks
Dr. E. G. Swem	Eva Atkinson
Mr. T. J. Stubs, Jr.	Robert Beeler
Elizabeth Lam	F. B. Glenn
E. P. Simpkins, Jr.	Elizabeth Pierce
Mary M. Land	Lillian Cossell
Helen Moore	S. A. Ozlin
Laura Calvin	G. M. Nolley
Mildred Cohen	Virginia Smith
Marjorie Lacy	Kathleen Cone

 **FEATURES**

MISTRESS MARY 1927

219

SPECIAL EVENTS OF THE YEAR

220

PROGRESS NUMBER

DRAMATICS

221

PROGRESS NUMBER

Boys' Glee Club

WILLIAM ATTKINSON	J. R. HOLT	MILTON SHREVES
ROBERT BARRETT	JESSE HOPKINS	S. STRADLEY
JOE BENNETT	WALLACE HICKS	JAMES STONE
CARROLL BROOKE	J. JOHNSON	ROBERT STEWART
L. F. BREWSTER	RICHARD LEE	WILLIAM VINCIENT
C. C. BROWN	MAXWELL LANIER	RAWLINGS WILLIAMS
EVERETT BUTLER	P. NORTON	TRUMAN WELLING
RUSSELL COLLINS	R. MEARS	JAMES WALLACE
W. E. CARMICHAEL	E. PARKER	LEONARD WHITEMORE
ERROLL DUNBAR	ROBERT PULLY	JOHN WARD
WILLARD ENTWISTLE	CLARENCE RIVES	JACK WHITE
KENNETH GRAHAM	DAVID STRAUGHN	HAYDEN RUSSELL

222

PROGRESS NUMBER

Girls' Glee Club

Elizabeth Allen	Margaret Fuller	Ruth Miller	Harriett Smith
Lucille Bidwell	Virginis Floyd	Lucille Morton	Katherine Seward
Mary Bullock	Eliza George	Elizabeth Moore	Olga Skore
Margaret Bilisoly	Frances Griffin	Mary Mayhew	Louise Stokes
Anne Bozarth	Margaret Hall	Hilda Miller	Mary Stern
Bernice Briggs	Edith Hollowell	Charlotte McKowan	Vera Trabold
Margretta Bloom	Mirilla Hicks	Virginia Moss	Virginia Turman
Doris Clarke	Margaret Howie	Mary Nininger	Elizabeth Trout
Grethe Christensen	Eliza Hunter	Virginia Paul	Mary G. Trout
Mary Christian	Frances Henry	Betty Powell	Page Vaughan
Catherine Carter	Betty Hugo	Blanche Pierce	Elizabeth Vaiden
Jane Currier	Caroline Hilliard	Peggy Parker	Julia Virner
Naomi Curtis	Ethel Hale	Alice Proudman	Grace Vipond
Isabelle Crigler	Helen Hostetler	Mary Quick	Elsie West
Kathleen Cone	Ruth James	Louise Rice	Lois Wilson
Mary Edgar	Lela Jackson	Dorothy Richardson	Edna Walters
Elizabeth Irwin	DeEtte Jones	Elizabeth Rowe	Louise White
Dorothy Farrar	Iola Johnson	Alice Ribble	Barta Worrell
Noma Fuqua	Anne Lindsey	Elizabeth Ryland	Edna Whitehurst
Rhoda Fry	Nan Langhorne	Mary Robertson	Indie Whitehurst
Bernice Ferguson	Betty Lanier	Lenore Schofield	Dorothy Wallace
Virginia Ford	Helen Lorenzen	Frances Shepherd	Elma Watkinson
			Virginia Williams

Who's

Terry Crossfield
CAPTAIN TENNIS

F. O. Clark
PRES. ATHLETIC COUNCIL

Dauba Green
EDITOR COLONIAL ECHO

Elizabeth Duke
PRES. GERMAN CLUB

Meb Davis
CAPTAIN FOOTBALL

Kenny Beatty
PRES. Y.M.C.A.

D. K. Van Wormer
EDITOR LITERARY MAGAZINE

Al Turner
MGR. FOOTBALL

Progress Number

Who

Granny Gresham
CAPTAIN CROSS COUNTRY

Bill Thompson
PRESIDENT HONOR COUNCIL

Bill Scott
PRES. FRESHMAN CLASS

Jessie James
EDITOR FLAT HAT

Suey Eason
CAPTAIN BASEBALL

Page Drinker
PRES. WOMENS STUDENT
GOVERNMENT

Yel Kent
PRES. SOPHOMORE CLASS

Allan Cooke
PRES. STUDENT BODY

Bill Elliott
PRES. SENIOR CLASS

225

The Indian Serenaders

ROBERT PULLY, *Director*
Piano

LESTER PHILLIPS   ROBERT PANNILL   CARY ZEHMER
First Saxophone   *Second Tenor Saxophone*   *Third Saxophone*

STANTON STRADLEY
Banjo

MANLEY MALLARD   JAMES GARRETT
Trumpet   *Trombone*

MILTON WHITE   THOMAS R. VARNEY
Traps   *Tuba*

226

Miss
Fairfax Griffith
May Queen

MAY DAY

Sponsors

Miss
Helen Wilcox
Sponsor–Student Body

Miss
Mary Love Davis
Sponsor—Senior Class

Miss
Fairfax Griffith
Sponsor of Colonial Echo

Miss
Katie S. Saxton
Sponsor—Literary Magazine

Miss
Lucille Parker
Sponsor–"Flat Hat"

Miss
Tilly Bell
Sponsor Y.M.C.A.

Miss
Doris Clark
Sponsor - Football

Miss
Margaret Towe
Sponsor Baseball

Miss
Kathleen Parrish
Sponsor - Basketball

Miss
Elizabeth Sencindiver
Sponsor ~ Track

Miss
Harriett Smith
Sponsor~Tennis

Miss
Patty Hunter
Sponsor, Athletic Council

Miss
Irma Hall
Sponsor - Cotillion Club

ACTIVITIES

INTERCOLLEGIATE DEBATE COUNCIL
Mr. Brooks, *Coach*

M. Weldon Thompson . . . . *President*   William Elliott . . . . *Manager*

Mr. G. H. Gelsinger   Dr. George W. Spicer   William B. Bolton   D. K. Van Wormer

VARSITY DEBATE TEAM

William H. Elliott   M. Weldon Thompson   George Hunt   Gordon Campbell
William B. Bolton   Edwin Lamberth   Arthur Kelsey   Lawrence Morscher
                                    Earl A. Garrett

FRESHMAN DEBATE TEAM

Milton Salasky   William R. Pretlow   Albert Cox

Philomathean Literary Society

ARTHUR, ROBERT	ELMORE, C. U.	LAND, K. S.
BEATTY, KENNETH	ENFIELD, R. F.	McKANN, P.
BREWSTER, L. F.	EPAMINANDO, J. F.	NEWBILL, PAGE
BROOKE, W. C.	FALES, E. D.	OBER, LEROY
BRADSHAW, H. C.	HANCOCK, J. H.	PARKER, B.
COOKE, BLACKNELL	HEALY, E.	MARSHALL, P.
COVINGTON, R. L.	HOLT. J. R.	QUESENBERRY, C. S.
DALTON, T. S.	JOHNSON, J. R. L.	RAILEY, J. R.
DIEBERT, J. H.	JOHNSON, J. A.	RANCHARD, WM.

REINACH, E. K.	TROMBLEY, W. A.
ROBERTSON, J. M.	TROTTER, LEIGH
SAVEDGE, W. R.	VINCIENT, WM.
SANGLER, H. M.	VAIDEN, R.
SAUNDERS, V.	REPASS, A.
STEWART, R. E.	MORECOCK, G.
SLAUGHTER, J. H.	WILCOX, F. S.
SPICER, H.	TRIBLE, W.
TURNER, C. A.	VAN WORMER, D. K.
TRICE, E. M.	ELLIOTT, W. H., JR.

PRINCE, LEON
BOWEN, J.
LE COMPT, FAY
WILKERSON, J. N.
WILKINSON, WM.
COLEMAN, W. A.
OVERSTREET, M.
WILLIAMS, S. O.
WALDEN, R. C.
SAVEDGE, J. R.
WEBB, E. G.
RINGLAND, WM.
DAVIS, M. C.
GREEN, J. B.

Officers

Donold Van Wormer
President First Term

Randolph Vaiden
President Second Term

First Term		*Second Term*
Randolph Vaiden	. . . . . *Vice-President*	Leroy Ober
Robert Covington	. . . . . *Secretary*	Sam Wilcox
Leroy Ober . . .	. . . . . *Treasurer*	J. R. L. Johnson
J. R. L. Johnson	. . . . *Sergeant-at-Arms*	Eliott Healy
H. A. McKann .	. . . . . *Chaplain*	W. A. Coleman
Wm. H. Elliott	. . . . . *Critic*	Wm. H. Elliott

THE SOCIETY

247

The Phoenix Literary Society

R. W. Brockwell	A. K. Hayward	Hugh Nelson
W. B. Bolton	H. V. Harrison	E. B. Novick
B. Burgwyn	C. M. Hailey	Ryland Nuckels
F. H. Beard	William Halpern	G. M. Nolley
C. Bussinger	J. B. Hopkins	S. A. Ozlin
C. W. Berry	P. B. Hamilton	W. R. Pretlow
W. J. Blair	H. J. Hancock	Ray Poole
P. B. Childress	J. J. Harrison, Jr.	W. A. Porter
J. W. Chambers	G. R. Hamner	N. Rittenberg
G. C. Cox	G. J. Haus	C. T. Rives
A. E. Cox	Garland Johnson	B. A. Riddle
C. Cushing	A. D. Johnson	E. Reynolds
T. Christie	H. T. Johnson	Louis Rotgin
C. E. Clevenger	C. C. Jones	E. C. Shortt
J. W. Calhoun	C. P. Jones	J. W. Stone
A. Cornell	R. R. Jones	M. C. Sammons
G. E. Campbell	E. C. Joyce	B. F. Spicer
Frank Davis	D. Arthur Kelsey	C. P. Scott
Stanley Fein	James Kelly	J. W. Shoemaker
Melvin Fields	E. Kerbawy	M. Solasky
A. E. Fryzell	James Lucy	J. C. Swanson
Walter Greenwood	Roger Klay	M. W. Thompson
R. Glasscock	John L. Lewis	Bernard Tankard
A. E. Garrett, Jr.	A. L. Lawrence	Swain Wool
W. R. Honover	J. F. McRae	W. B. Attkinson
E. Hallam	R. Moses	W. M. Entwistle
E. H. Hill	L. N. Moscher	T. M. Carter
	Rev. H. P. Mileer	

PROGRESS NUMBER

COLONIAL ECHO

Officers

JONES
President First Term

HILL
President Second Term

First Term		Second Term
EDWARD HILL	*Vice-President*	MELVIN FIELDS
ARTHUR KELSEY	*Secretary*	JOHN C. SWANSON
	Program Secretary	E. A. GARRETT, JR.
E. A. GARRETT	*Treasurer*	ARTHUR KELSEY
JOHN C. SWANSON	*Sergeant-at-Arms*	JAMES LUCY

THE SOCIETY

249

PROGRESS NUMBER

Y. M. C. A. CABINET

PROGRESS NUMBER

Women's Debate Council and Team

Mr. Brooks, *Faculty Advisor*

Helen Moffet
Manager

Evelyn Steele
Treasurer

Constance Jamieson

Irella Lawson

Margaret Morris

Miriam Silberger

Virginia Nicholas

Katheryn Topping

J. Leslie Hall Literary Society

ADAMS, IRMA	DOUGLAS, BETTY	LAND, MARY	RATHEIN, DORIS
ADDIS, ALICE	DAVIS, MILDRED	LEVY, CECILIA	ROBINSON, LAURENA
ALEXANDER, VIRGINIA	DAVIS, MAY	LORENZO, HELEN	REESE, DOT
ALLEN, ELIZABETH	DIGGS, MARY	LANKFORT, DOT	RICHARDSON, EDITH
AMBLER, ELIZABETH	EVERHART, ROSA	LA RUE, MARION	ROWE, ELIZABETH
ATKINSON, EVA	ERWIN, ELIZABETH	LANIER, ELIZABETH	RHODES, DOT
ANDREWS, RUTH	EGGLESTON, MARGARET	LANING, MARION	ROBERTSON, MARY
BALLARD, GRACE	ENNIS, VIRNELLE	LINDSEY, ANNE	SAUNDERS, LINDA
BROWN, IVA	EDGAR, MARY	LAVENSTEIN, LEE	SAVAGE, MARTHA
BAILEY, MARGARET	FORD, VIRGINIA	LAM, CATHERINE	STOKES, LOUISE
BLACKWELL, E.	FULLER, MARGARET	MONTEIRO, HELEN	SOUTHERLAND, DAISEY
BARKER, SUE	FINNEY, MILLISEN	McKAWN, CHARLOTTE	SEWARD, KATHERYN
BRITTINGHAM, AGNES	FARINHOLT, VIRGINIA	MOORE, ANN	SKORA, OLGA
BLAKE, ANN	FORBES, JUANILA	MARSHALL, MARGARET	SARGENT, MARION
BILISOLY, MARGARET	FIELDS, LAURA	MILLER, RUTH	SPITAL, NELLIE
BERRY, EVELYN	FERGUSON, BINNIE	MORRISON, MARY	SWIFT, PAULINE
BRENNER, MARGARET	FLEET, MARY	MESSICK, ANNE	SLOUGH, LOUISE
BIDWELL, LUCILLE	GOODWIN, NORVELLE	MORTON, LUCY	SMITH, PAULINE
BENNETT, CARLYN	GRESHAM, MARTHA	McELROY, KATHERINE	SMYRE, MARGARET
BOSWELL, LUCY	GOULDMAN, VIRGINIA	MILLER, MARGARET	SHIRLEY, GENE
BANKS, JEWELL	GRAZZ, EVA	MOFFETT, HELEN	STERN, RUTH
BALL, REBECCA	GOUGH, ISABEL	MORTON, MABELE	SEAMAN, RUTH
BLUME, MARGARETTA	GRIFFIN, ELIZABETH	MORTON, LUCY	SLEMP, MARGARET
BURGWYN, FRANCES	GLOCKER, ELIZABETH	MILLER, LUCY	STINNETT, THELMA
BEEBE, VERNETTE	GLENN, KATHERINE	MILEY, CHARLOTTE	SCHULTZ, BARBARA
CLARKE, VIRGINIA	HUNT, MARY	MARGOLIS, HANNAH	SHEREN, CARRIE
CRABTREE, VIRGINIA	HANCOCK, CORINNE	MELTON, VIRGINIA	SMITH, ELEANOR
CACCOPPI, ANNE	HUGO, ELIZABETH	MILLER, MARION	TRABOLD, VERA
CALURA, LUCILLE	HALL, OLIVIA	NOTTINGHAM, LUCY	TICER, ELLEN
CANEK, THERESA	HUGHES, NAOMI	NUNN, ETHEL	TOPPING, KITTY
CORNICK, SUE	HULL, VIRGINIA	NELSON, VIRGINIA	TANNER, ELIZABETH
COOK, CATHERINE	HICKS, MARILLA	NICHOLAS, KATHERINE	THOMPSON, CHRIS
COLBURN, EDNA	HOLLIGAN, DOROTHY	NICHOLSON, BETTY	TRENT, ELIZABETH
CHAPLAIN, MARGARET	HOGGE, HELEN	NEALE, EVELYN	TAYLOR, CORNELIA
CHRISTIAN, MARGARET	HAYNES, EVELYN	ORBACH, SYLVIA	TROUT, ELIZABETH
COLEY, JANE	HANDY, MARION	OBER, MARJORIE	VAUGHAN, ELEANOR
COLEY, LENORE	HUNDLEY, ANNETTE	ORANGE, IRMA	WARING, EMMA
CARPENTER, SUSIE	HUGHES, SARAH	PENDLETON, CATHERINE	WARING, MARTHA
CRAWFORD, VIRGINIA	HOSTETLER, ELLEN	PIFER, HELEN	WHITEHURST, INDIE
CHICK, FLORENCE	HARRIS, MARJORIE	PORTER, HELEN	WIGGLESWORTH, OLIVE
CHEYNE, MARION	HUNTER, KATHARYN	PAYNE, CARRIE	WARD, FRANCES
CONE, KATHLEEN	HOLE, DOROTHY	PALMER, CLARE	WARE, MARY
CLARK, DORIS	HOUGH, ELIZABETH	PENN, SARAH	WORTHINGTON, JANE
CURTIS, NAOMI	JOHNSON, BROOKS	PIERCE, BLANCHE	WAY, ELIZABETH
COTHRAN, CATHERINE	JOHNSON, MARGARET	PILCHER, LOUISE	WHITE, CAROLINE
DABNEY, FLORENCE	JACKSON, LELIA	POWELL, ELIZABETH	WEILAND, VIRGINIA
DUNLAP, ELIZABETH	JOHNSTON, MURIEL	PARMER, EMMA	WILLIAMS, VIRGINIA
DAVIS, CARRIE	JAMIESON, CONSTANCE	PAGE, CONSTANCE	WALKER, ALENE
DIFFIN, MARGARET	JONES, VIRGINIA	REID, AMY	WARD, MARY
DUNLAP, MARGARET	KING, GENE	ROWE, HAWSIE	WATKINSON, ALMA
DENISON, LORNA	KAHLE, KATHERINE	RIBBLE, MARY	WALLACE, DOROTHY
DOWN, DOROTHY	LOVELACE, ALMA	ROUNTREE, JEAN	WEBB, ROSELYN
DRINKER, PAGE	LOWE, ESTHER	REYNOLDS, CATHERINE	WILSON, LINDA
DU BRAY, LEONA	LANE, LOUISE	RICE, LOUISE	WITHROW, CLARA
			ZIGLER, CHARLOTTE

YOST, MARGUERITE   YANCEY, FLORENCE

STINNETT   FARINHOLT   SHELTON   BILISOLY

OFFICERS OF THE SOCIETY

VIRGINIA FARINHOLT . . . . *President*

WILLIE SHELTON . . . . *Vice-President*

MARGARET BILISOLY . . . . *Secretary*

THELMA STINNETT . . . . *Treasurer*

THE SOCIETY

253

Elizabeth Lam
PRESIDENT

Phyllis Logan
VICE-PRESIDENT

Betsy R. Nickolson
SECRETARY

Willie Shelton
TREASURER

Marjorie Lacy
PROGRAM CHAIRMAN

Mary Ribble
SOCIAL CHAIRMAN

Frances Gordon
WORLD FELLOWSHIP
CHAIRMAN

Kathleen Cone
PUBLICITY CHAIRMAN

Melba Gravely
MUSIC CHAIRMAN

Edith Dodd
DEVOTIONAL CHAIRMAN

Katherine Glenn
GIRLS RESERVE
CHAIRMAN

Y. W. C. A. CABINET

PROGRESS NUMBER

Student
Government

J. ALAN COOK
President Student Body

PAGE DRINKER
President Women's Student Government

257

Honor Council

WILLIAM G. THOMPSON
President

MELVIN C. DAVIS
Vice-President

J. M. HURT   JAMES WALLACE
EDWARD JUSTIS   JOHN WATERS
CHARLES CHANDLER

Senior-Junior Tribunal

Melvin C. Davis
Chairman

Alan Cook   E. T. Justis
E. C. Macon   E. A. Smith
George P. Porter

259

Executive Council

PAGE DRINKER . . . . *President*
LAURA WHITEHEAD . . . . *First Vice-President*
POLLY VENABLE . . . . *Second Vice-President*
POLLY HINES . . . . *Secretary*
ELIZABETH VAIDEN . . . . *Treasurer*

FRANCES GORDON   NANCY BURKE
HARRIET ZIMMERMAN   ELIZABETH SEXTON
ELIZABETH JOHNSON

Judicial Council

LAURA WHITEHEAD   KATHERINE RHODES
President   *Secretary*

RUTH JAMES   GRACE MILLER   KATHERINE COOK
ALICE CHEWNING   KATHERYN TOPPING   KATHERINE LAM
               MARGARET HOWIE
               REID WEST

Theta Alpha Phi

MISS ALTHEA HUNT   POLLY VENABLE
GEORGE REILLY   PHYLLIS LOGAN
D. K. VAN WORMER   SAMUEL STAPLES

DRAMATIC CLUB

MISS ALTHEA HUNT, *Faculty Adviser*

MARTHA CLAIBORNE   GEORGE SINON
POLLY HINES   WELDON THOMPSON
PHYLLIS LOGAN   WILLIAM VINCENT
LUCILLE PARKER   NATHAN CAFFEE
NOMA FUQUA   GRACE MILLER
SAM STAPLES   LOIS LACY
UPTON THOMAS   GERTRUDE HENDERSON
D. K. VAN WORMER   PEGGY HALL
POLLY VENABLE   EDITH DODD
TRUMAN WELLING   STANLEY FEIN
ARTHUR KELSEY   LENORE SCHOFIELD
RAY POOLE   HELEN HOSTETLER

HONORARY OR ASSOCIATE MEMBERS

MISS SELLEVOLD   MR. BROOKS
MRS. HIPP   MR. REILLY

PROGRESS NUMBER

Publications

The Colonial Echo

WILLIAM C. LINN
Editor-in-Chief
First Term

JOHN B. GREEN
Editor-in-Chief
Second Term

KENNETH B. BEATTY
Business Manager

THE STAFF

NATHAN CAFFEE . . . . *Managing Editor*
POLLY HINES . . . . *Associate Editor*
BETSY PRICE . . . . *Associate Editor*
GARLAND JOHNSON . . . . *Activities Editor*
SARA EVERETT . . . . *Activities Editor*
ALICE CHEWNING . . . . *Athletic Editor*
EDWARD FALES . . . . *Athletic Editor*
MARTHA CLAIBORNE . . . . *Art Editor*
VIRGINIA FARINHOLT . . . . *Art Editor*
HAYDEN RUSSELL . . . . *Fraternity Editor*
PHYLLIS LOGAN . . . . *Fraternity Editor*
BERT LUDLOW . . . . . *Assistant Advertising Manager*

264

Polly Hines
ASSOCIATE EDITOR

Nathan Caffee
MANAGING EDITOR

James Robertson
ADVERTISING MGR.

Garland Johnson
ACTIVITIES EDITOR

George R. Mapp
PHOTOGRAPH EDITOR

Sara A. Everett
ACTIVITIES EDITOR

Bert Ludlow
ASS'T ADVERTISING MGR.

Martha Claiborne
ART EDITOR

Alice Chewning
SPORTS EDITOR

Phyllis Logan
FRATERNITY EDITOR

PROGRESS NUMBER

The Flat Hat

WILLARD N. JAMES
Editor-in-Chief

JOHN ETHERIDGE
Business Manager

THE STAFF

ARTHUR P. HENDERSON . . . . *Managing Editor*
EDWARD D. FALES, JR. . . . . *Associate Editor*
MARY RIBBLE . . . . *Associate Editor*
JOHN B. GREEN . . . . *Alumni Editor*
BARTON D. PATTIE . . . . *Sports Editor*
FLOYD A. GESSFORD . . . . *Statistician*
LLOYD WILLIAMS . . . . . *Assistant Sports Editor*
CATHERINE COTHRAN . . . . . *Assistant Sports Editor*
BILL LAWRENCE . . . . *Feature Writer*

OFFICE MEN

M. WELDON THOMPSON   ROBERT DOYLE   BOYD CARTER

REPORTERS

DEETTE JONES   WILLIAM S. VINCENT
PEGGY NININGER   PAUL NORTON
LUCY NOTTINGHAM   WILLIAM ROUNTREE
HARRIET SMITH   RALPH HINMAN

MACON SAMMONS, *Assistant Business Manager*

ALBERT VALISKA, *Circulation Manager*

PROGRESS NUMBER

L. W. I'Anson
BUSINESS MANAGER

John B. Green
ALUMNI EDITOR

M. W. Thompson
OFFICE MAN

Floyd Gessford
SPORTS STATISTICIAN

Boyd Carter
OFFICE MAN

Robert Doyle
OFFICE MAN

B. D. Pattie
SPORTS EDITOR

Ashby Lawrence
FEATURE WRITER

Macon Sammons
ASS'T BUSINESS MGR

A. P. Henderson
MANAGING EDITOR

Mary Ribble
ASSOCIATE EDITOR

PROGRESS NUMBER

The Literary Magazine

W. C. West
Business Manager

D. K. Van Wormer
Editor-in-Chief

Editorial Staff

Robert S. Barrett
Managing Editor

Associate Editors

Samuel Staples
Hannah Margolis

Mary Matthew
Harriett Smith

Business Staff

Algenon K. Turner
Circulation Manager

McLain T. O'Ferrall
Assistant Business Manager

PROGRESS NUMBER

269

PROGRESS NUMBER

The Straw Hat

M. Weldon Thompson, *Editor-in-Chief*   George Morecock, *Business Manager*

Published Weekly, Summer Session, 1927

Nathan M. Caffee . . . . *Managing Editor*

W. E. Evenson . . . . *Circulation Manager*

Barton D. Pattie	Mary Ribble
William S. Vincent	Billie Shelton
D. Arthur Kelsey	Stanley Fein
L. L. Born	M. B. Schwetz

PROGRESS NUMBER

 **ATHLETICS**

The Varsity Club

M. C. DAVIS, *President*

ARTHUR MATSU	R. C. POWER	A. A. WALDRUTH
CARLTON MACON	WELDON BLOXOM	PAUL BALDACCI
ALAN COOK	EDWARD JUSTIS	HARRY PAXSON
WILLIAM ELLIOTT	WARFIELD WINN	RALPH FERRANDINI
DAUBA GREEN	LELAND WALKER	JAMES WALLACE
A. K. TURNER	GIDEON TODD	IRVING DAVIS
KENNETH BEATTY	LOGAN HUDSON	GORDON CAMPBELL
WILLIAM LINN	C. R. THOMAS	Y. O. KENT
MERRILL EASON	R. W. DURHAM	WILLIAM FIELDS
LOWELL AYRES	JOHN SAURBAUN	WILLIAM CARMICHAEL
H. C. SOMERS	T. BAUSERMAN	M. MOZELESKI
M. T. O'FERRELL	HORACE TAYLOR	HARRY LIGHT
GREYSON DAUGHTERY	MACHIEL MAISTER	ABE SILVERMAN
GRANVILLE GRESHAM	GEORGE NOFAL	WILLIAM SCOTT
	JAMES MURPHY	

IN FACULTY

J. C. CHANDLER	G. E. GREGORY	J. B. TODD

PROGRESS NUMBER

Men's Athletic Council

F. O. CLARK . . . . *President*
E. CARLTON MACON . . . . *Vice-President*
ROBERT BARRETT . . . . *Secretary-Treasurer*

WILLIAM G. THOMPSON
ALGERNON K. TURNER
W. J. BLACKWELL

Football

▯ FOOTBALL ▯

Tasker, *Coach*

Todd, *Assistant Coach*

Davis *Captain*

Viewed from the standpoint of actual field victories the 1927 football season of William and Mary would not be judged a crowning success. To those, however, who were acquainted with the handicaps the team had to overcome and who witnessed the efforts of Coach Tasker and Captain Davis to build up a new fighting machine, the season was highly satisfactory. When the season opened the coaches were faced with the problem of assimilating new material and the residue of what in recent years had been a heavy team.

The team lost the first two games, and tied the Thanksgiving Day game with Richmond, but mid-season clashes were marked by constant good playing.

The Varsity Squad

276

⃗ FOOTBALL ⃗

MACON

EASON

COOK

CATHOLIC U., 12; WILLIAM AND MARY, 0
SEPTEMBER 24TH

This hard-fought game inaugurated the use of the new lights on Cary field and introduced night football in the East. The largest crowd that ever witnessed a football game at Williamsburg saw Catholic University hammer its way down the field twice for touchdowns. Captain Davis and Bloxom, the "midget back," featured for the Indians.

SYRACUSE, 18; WILLIAM AND MARY, 0
OCTOBER 1ST

An unfortunate slip in the Indians attack in the first quarter gave Syracuse a "love game," and for the fifth successive time the Orangemen emerged victorious over the Taskerites. Fighting under a boiling sun, William and Mary outplayed Syracuse in the first quarter

Macon Through Chattanooga's Line

277

⌑ FOOTBALL ⌑

ELLIOTT

BLOXOM

TAYLOR

and advanced the ball to their opponent's five-
yard line, but were thrown for a twenty-yard
loss on the fourth down. The quarter ended
without a score. In the second quarter, Bar-
buti, an old scorer against the Indians, swung
into action, and the Northerners scored three
times before the game was finished.

LENOIR-RHYNE, 0; WILLIAM AND MARY, 19
OCTOBER 8TH

A deluging rainstorm that blurred the flood
lights and turned Cary field into a sea of mud
failed to dampen the ardor of a large crowd
that saw William and Mary wallow, dive and
all but swim to a victory over the Wildcats
from North Carolina. The end of the first
half brought a heavier downfall of rain, but
a loyal throng of students remained to watch,
cheer and shiver through a scoreless second
half.

Darden Through Hampden-Sydney

COLONIAL ECHO

ⅠⅠ FOOTBALL ⅠⅠ

CARMICHAEL

BAUSERMAN

MOZELESKI

QUANTICO, 20; WILLIAM AND MARY, 14
OCTOBER 15TH

In what was probably the hardest and best fought game of the season the Indians administered a scare to the unbeaten "Devil Dogs" and smeared their clean record with two touchdowns. The Marines scored the deciding touchdown in the second half when William and Mary was penalized to the one-foot line.

CONCORD STATE, 7; WILLIAM AND MARY, 13
OCTOBER 22ND

William and Mary literally ran away with the game in the second half and emerged victorious from the last night game of the season. Concord's single touchdown was scored in the first half before the Varsity and relieved the second string men, who had started the game.

Scott Around Richmond's End

279

PROGRESS NUMBER

" FOOTBALL "

FIELDS

MEISTER

WALDRUTH

PRINCETON, 35; WILLIAM AND MARY, 7
OCTOBER 29TH

Although the Indians lost they repeated, to some extent, the performance against the Marines, and twisted the Tiger's tail for the first touchdown of the season in Palmer stadium. The Indians' weakness lay chiefly in their constant fumbling.

CHATTANOOGA, 12; WILLIAM AND MARY, 7
NOVEMBER 5TH

A large crowd of students went to Norfolk and saw Maister catch a beautiful low pass and run twenty yards for a touchdown. The Indians might have scored another in the first quarter, but the old fumbling weakness cropped out again, and so close to the goal line that the ball rolled over only to have a Moccasin recover and bring it out.

Bauserman Stops Hampden-Sydney

PROGRESS NUMBER

" FOOTBALL "

Paxton

Nofal

Scott

Roanoke, 7; William and Mary, 18
November 11th

The Indians invaded Roanoke Armistice Day and charged with a rush into their first state game. The opening attack netted three first downs and wound up in a touchdown. In the second quarter Roanoke resorted to baffling passes, scored and kicked the goal, taking the lead. The Indians retaliated in full force in the last quarter with two touchdowns. No goals were kicked.

Richmond, 0; William and Mary, 0.
November 24th

The old hoodoo that has kept William and Mary from ever taking more than four successive victories from Richmond seemed to have

Freshmen on Cary Field at Catholic U. Game

" FOOTBALL "

Darden

Turner, *Manager*

Murphy

full play Thanksgiving Day when the Indians invaded Richmond, apparently set for victory. The game ended without a touchdown for either side, although the Taskerites had put the ball over twice in rapid succession. The first touchdown proved to be barely a few inches out of bounds, and the second, immediately afterward, was ineffective because one player was off-side.

This game marked the passing from the gridiron of four William and Mary athletes: Captain Davis, Eason, Elliott and Cook. All have served for four years and they will leave shoes hard to fill in the seasons to come.

Indians vs. Moccasins

PROGRESS NUMBER

Basketball

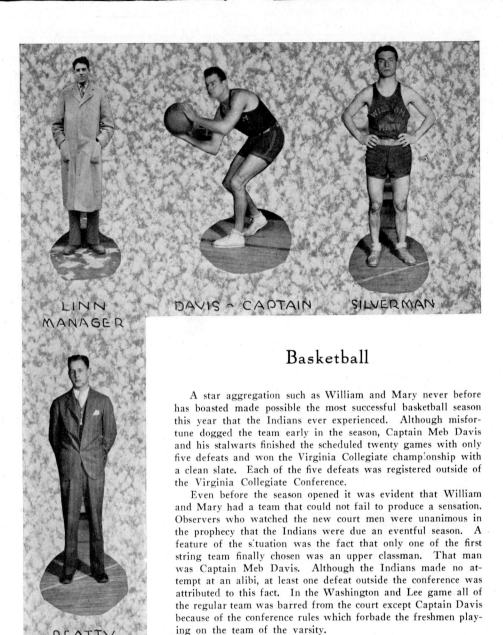

LINN
MANAGER

DAVIS ~ CAPTAIN

SILVERMAN

BEATTY
MANAGER ~

Basketball

A star aggregation such as William and Mary never before has boasted made possible the most successful basketball season this year that the Indians ever experienced. Although misfortune dogged the team early in the season, Captain Meb Davis and his stalwarts finished the scheduled twenty games with only five defeats and won the Virginia Collegiate champ¦onship with a clean slate. Each of the five defeats was registered outside of the Virginia Collegiate Conference.

Even before the season opened it was evident that William and Mary had a team that could not fail to produce a sensation. Observers who watched the new court men were unanimous in the prophecy that the Indians were due an eventful season. A feature of the s¦tuation was the fact that only one of the first string team finally chosen was an upper classman. That man was Captain Meb Davis. Although the Indians made no attempt at an alibi, at least one defeat outside the conference was attributed to this fact. In the Washington and Lee game all of the regular team was barred from the court except Captain Davis because of the conference rules which forbade the freshmen playing on the team of the varsity.

Features of the season were the double defeat of the University of Richmond, an accomplishment wh¦ch few William and Mary teams have been able to boast of, and the high point scor-

LIGHT   SAUERBRUN   MOZELESKI

FARRANDINI

ing of Abe Silverman, who is a star forward. Early in January Richmond came to Williamsburg and went home defeated. Later in the month Coach Tasker's men went to Richmond and defeated the Spiders on their home court.

Silverman achieved the distinction of high point scoring for the state and had a total of 225 points to his credit. He and Ralph Ferrandini led the Indian scorers—Ferrandini had second place with a score of 110 points, and Mozeleski had third place.

In December the Indians made their first trip and were defeated by the Catholic University and the Naval Academy. The defeats showed the team its weaknesses at the beginning of the season, and by the time the Indians were ready for the second trip, which was in the first week of January, Coach Tasker had built up his uncertain spots. The second trip brought better results. The Indian team beat Hampden-Sidney, Roanoke, and Lynchburg, but lost to Washington and Lee.

When the Indians beat Richmond, January 17, they were accorded the third place in the state, the University of Virginia and Washington and Lee holding first and second places respectively. By January 20 Silverman was showing the form that later produced such a sensation, and he had up to that time scored eighty-eight points. Previously he had thirty out of thirty-four fouls. Ferrandini had assumed second place with fifty-two points, and Davis and Light had tied for third place, each having thirty-two points. After the January exams the team launched into its most strenuous week, trimming Emory and Henry, Stevens Tech, Wake Forest and Richmond, all in rapid

PROGRESS NUMBER

succession. In the series of games each of the five first men showed up to full worth, and all men were praised by the press and fans for skillful court work.

By February 10, Silverman had scored 118, and writers unofficially accorded him first place in the state. Ferrandini was running second at William and Mary with seventy-five. In the next two weeks Silverman was to run up more than one hundred additional baskets.

The third trip, early in February, carried the team into North Carolina, where they were to receive another defeat at the hands of Guilford. This was offset, however, by victories over Wake Forest and Elon.

The following week, being the last of the season, witnessed two big games. On one night the team took revenge on Guilford, and in the last game of the year swamped Brooklyn Polytechnic Institute 50 to 19.

The season centered the attention of Virginia sports writers on the fast Indian quintet, all of whom, with the exception of Captain Davis, are expected to play again next fall under the captaincy of "Waffles" Winn. All of William and Mary's players, first and second string alike, received the accord of the sports observers. The freshman team, which will have valuable material for the coming year, completed a successful season. The total Indian score in the 1927-1928 season was 692 as against 545 scored by opponents.

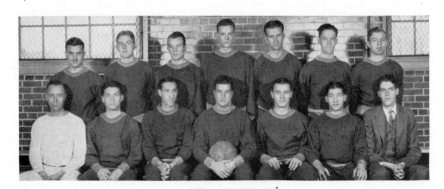

THE VARSITY SQUAD

Baseball

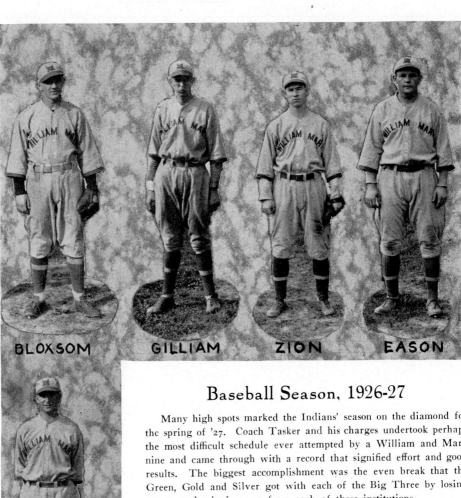

BLOXSOM   GILLIAM   ZION   EASON

AYERS

Baseball Season, 1926-27

Many high spots marked the Indians' season on the diamond for the spring of '27. Coach Tasker and his charges undertook perhaps the most difficult schedule ever attempted by a William and Mary nine and came through with a record that signified effort and good results. The biggest accomplishment was the even break that the Green, Gold and Silver got with each of the Big Three by losing one to and winning one from each of these institutions.

The first of the year presented the great problem of building up a team around the very few veterans who had returned, but the end of the season found the locals possessing a well rounded nine of exceptional ability on the field and at the bat. Captain Thompson, Bloxom and Ayers of the infield, and Eason of the outer garden, and Stickle and Taylor from the pitching staff were the only veterans returning. The remainder of the team was picked from the previous year's freshman team and new men in college.

The season opened with a great victory over Yale in a game which boasted of a most dramatic climax. Every spectator will remember Eason's home run in the ninth frame that clinched the victory. The next contest on the home grounds went to Holy Cross, although the locals well outhit the visitors. Harvard and Prince-

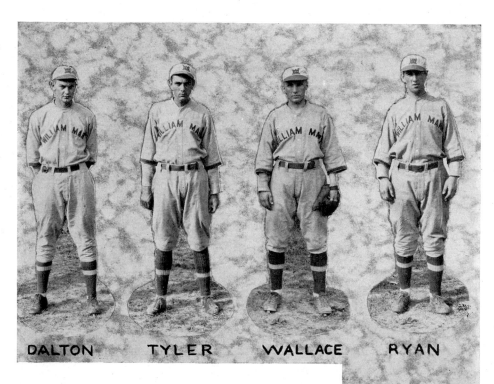

DALTON   TYLER   WALLACE   RYAN

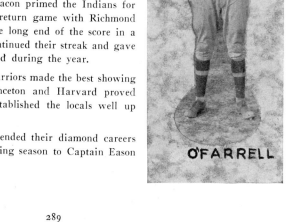

O'FARRELL

ton, however, took two games in rapid succession but left the Indians primed for two gridiron opponents—Syracuse and Lynchburg. Jim Wallace held the former to one hit for a victory, and Eason's bat routed the latter to set the Indians on their feet again. A severe drubbing for the Randolph Macon Yellow Jackets was the next accomplishment of the tribe.

The Richmond jinx again manifested itself and the Spiders succeeded in rapping the Indian nine in the first game of a two-game series. Another win over Randolph Macon primed the Indians for revenge, and revenge they got in the return game with Richmond on Cary Field when the Tribe took the long end of the score in a closely contested fray. Wake Forest continued their streak and gave the Indians the worst drubbing received during the year.

On the annual Northern trip the Warriors made the best showing of the year. Return games with Princeton and Harvard proved profitable to the Indian cause, and established the locals well up in the world of baseball.

Captain Thompson and Mac Zion ended their diamond careers and handed over the hopes of the coming season to Captain Eason and his teammates.

PROGRESS   NUMBER

CAPT.-THOMPSON   COACH-TASKER   MANAGER-ZOLLINGER

Baseball Results, 1927

William and Mary	3;	Yale	3
William and Mary	1;	Holy Cross	6
William and Mary	7;	Syracuse	0
William and Mary	9;	Harvard	11
William and Mary	7;	Princeton	10
William and Mary	9;	Lynchburg	8
William and Mary	24;	Randolph-Macon	8
William and Mary	1;	Richmond	4
William and Mary	13;	Randolph-Macon	1
William and Mary	9;	Harvard	8
William and Mary	2;	Yale	3
William and Mary	2;	Holy Cross	6
William and Mary	6;	Princeton	2

THE VARSITY SQUAD

PROGRESS NUMBER

Track

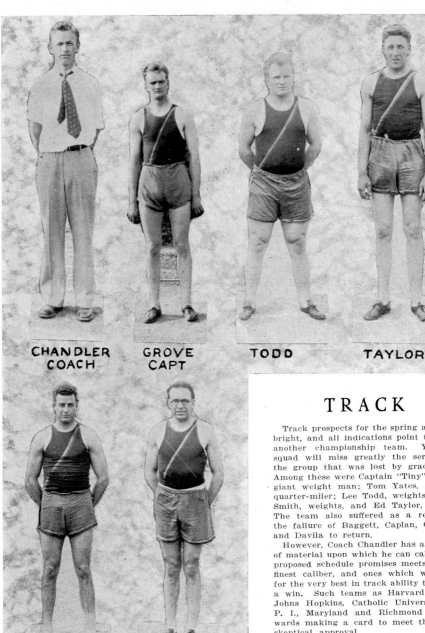

CHANDLER COACH — GROVE CAPT — TODD — TAYLOR

DAVIS — SMITH

TRACK

Track prospects for the spring are very bright, and all indications point towrads another championship team. Yet the squad will miss greatly the service of the group that was lost by graduation. Among these were Captain "Tiny" Grove, giant weight man; Tom Yates, sterling quarter-miler; Lee Todd, weights; Spike Smith, weights, and Ed Taylor, jumps. The team also suffered as a result of the failure of Baggett, Caplan, Graham and Davila to return.

However, Coach Chandler has a wealth of material upon which he can call. The proposed schedule promises meets of the finest caliber, and ones which will call for the very best in track ability to claim a win. Such teams as Harvard, Navy, Johns Hopkins, Catholic University, V. P. I., Maryland and Richmond go towards making a card to meet the most skeptical approval.

From the last years varsity the mentors have a number of seasoned veterans. Captain Meb Davis still exhibits old form on the hurdles and in the jumps. As usual he can be depended on to come

CAPLAN   YATES   JUSTIS   MANAGER-TERRY

GREEN   CAMPBELL

through right up in front. The other letter men who have returned are Davis, Green, Gresham, Daughtery, Campbell, Kent, Thomas and Justis.

In the dashes Green and Davis are on hand with assistance from several freshmen of promise. The middle distances will be well taken care of by Daughtery and Gresham, with Babb, from last year's frosh squad, as understudy.

The distance runs should not trouble Coach Chandler, for Campbell, with much freshman auxiliary force, is again on hand. The hurdles and jumps find Thomas and Davis back with Kent and Durham vaulting in old style. Ed Justis is the only letter man handling the field events, but available material is on hand from the squad of last year.

The 1927 season ended very successfully for the Indians. By virtue of wins over Richmond and Randolph Macon the locals established just claims to the state Class B title. Unless some unforeseen circumstance intervenes and upsets the regular course of events, the team of 1928 will repeat.

Mention should be made of the Cross-Country and Relay teams. Both are continuing successful and add victory after victory to their records.

PROGRESS NUMBER

KENT   GRAHAM   DAVIS   DAVILA   GRESHAM   BAGGETT

The Team, 1927

D. G. Grove, *Captain*	*Weights*
L. B. Todd	*Weights*
Ed Taylor	*Jumps*
M. C. Davis	*Hurdles*
Callie Smith	*Weights*
J. B. Green	*Dashes*
I. Davis	*Dashes*
J. T. Yates	*Quarter-Mile*
G. Gresham	*Half-mile*
F. Graham	*Half-mile*
Gorden Campbell	*Two-mile*
J. Caplan	*Two-mile*
Ed Justis	*Javelin*
M. Baggett	*Hurdles*
J. Davila	*Jumps*
Y. O. Kent	*Pole-vault*

THE RELAY TEAM

PROGRESS NUMBER

Minor Sports

Tennis Team

TERRY CROSSFIELD, *Captain*	W. N. JAMES, *Manager*
LEROY OBER	RICHARD HOWARD
JOHN LEWIS	FRANK WIGGINS

The Cross-Country Team

GRANVILLE GRESHAM, *Captain*	L. W. I'ANSON, *Manager*
GILLEY	NELSON
SPICER	VERNON
CAMPBELL	HUDSON

PROGRESS NUMBER

Swimming Team

E. T. JUSTIS, *Captain*   RAY POOLE, *Manager*

PHILLIPS	THOMPSON	RODGERS
VAN PUTTEN	SWEM	CHASE
MURPHY	LEACH	WOOD
VAN WORMER	PORTER	COVINGTON
	BUTLER	

Wrestling Team

WELTON BLOXOM, *Captain*   W. B. BOLTON, *Manager*

GARRARD	McRAE	ROBERTS
ENFIELD	PAXON	VERNON
CRIGLER	EASON	FRYZELL
	CONSTANTINO	

PROGRESS NUMBER

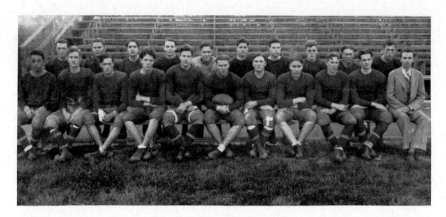

FRESHMAN FOOTBALL SQUAD

FRESHMAN BASKETBALL SQUAD

Women's Athletics

The Athletic Council

L. Tucker Jones	Elizabeth Duke	Nancy Burke	Lucy Pilcher
Chairman	*President*	*Treasurer*	*Secretary*

Martha Barksdale
Margurite Wynne-Roberts

The Monogram Club

Nancy Burke, *President*

Harriett Zimmerman	Genevieve Hoffman	Gene Miles	Charlotte King
Elizabeth Tanner	Alice Chewning	Polly Hines	Curle Sinclair
Rosa Flannery	Lena Deshazo	Dot Langford	Agnes Winn
Brownie Osmond	Laura Fields	Helen Maffett	Edith Wilkins
Laura Whitehead	Anne Fiddler	Virginia Buston	Virginia Harper

300

The Hockey Team

KING	*Left Wing*
TANNER	*Left Inside*
SINCLAIR	*Center Forward*
DESHAZO	*Right Inside*
FIDDLER	*Right Wing*
ZIMMERMAN (C)	*Left Half*
CHEWNING	*Center Half*
HOFMAN	*Right Half*
MILES	*Left Back*
OSMOND	*Right Back*
BUSTON	*Right Back*
MAFFETT	*Goal Keeper*

The Season's Results

William and Mary	1;	Sweet Briar	10
William and Mary	9;	Farmville	4
William and Mary	6;	George Washington	2
William and Mary	1;	New York University (tie)	1

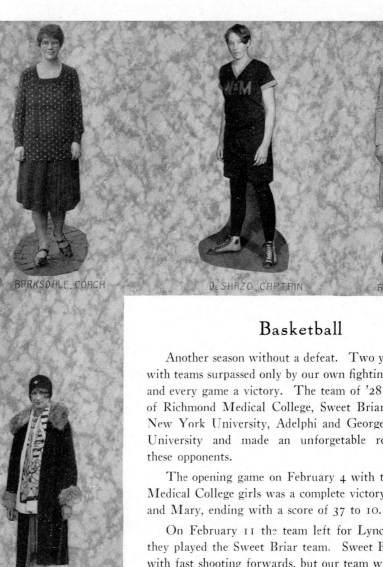

BARKSDALE, COACH   DeSHAZO, CAPTAIN   ROBERTS, COACH

HARPER, MANAGER

Basketball

Another season without a defeat. Two years of games with teams surpassed only by our own fighting Indianettes, and every game a victory. The team of '28 met the girls of Richmond Medical College, Sweet Briar, Lynchburg, New York University, Adelphi and George Washington University and made an unforgetable record against these opponents.

The opening game on February 4 with the Richmond Medical College girls was a complete victory for William and Mary, ending with a score of 37 to 10.

On February 11 the team left for Lynchburg, where they played the Sweet Briar team. Sweet Briar came up with fast shooting forwards, but our team was inspired by the tireless fight of our guards and played up to a score of 34 to 20. The work and strain of the game was easily forgotten in the pleasure of the royal entertainment given our team by the Sweet Briar girls on that evening.

Back again on the home floor on February 18, playing

PROGRESS NUMBER

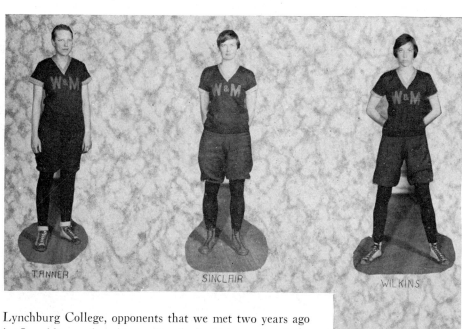

TANNER   SINCLAIR   WILKINS

Lynchburg College, opponents that we met two years ago in Lynchburg, the old varsity checked the rush of the Lynchburg six by their skill and speed. The final score was: William and Mary 34, Lynchburg 23.

Then the much planned for Northern trip. New York bound, March 3, and we crashed through Adelphi with another victory though the game was a little slow and stiff in comparison with the previous games with Adelphi.

Sunday in New York didn't seem to cramp the team's style, and though the overwhelming last year's score of 47 to 15 was a thing of the past, on Monday 5 we led New York University again by a score of 30 to 28. The game was made even more interesting by the cheers of William and Mary alumni now on the New York University faculty.

Last, but not least, the memorable George Washington University game on our home floor March 17. We'll never forget it. The work of our guards was nothing short of magnificent, and the unfailing captain, Lena

WINN

PROGRESS NUMBER

BURKE   DUKE

DeShazo, with her hard playing and her beautiful shooting totaled her season's goals for 112 points by bringing up the score with the help of her team to 29 to 26, with William and Mary on top. The playing of the George Washington team was of a very high order, and we consider this victory the greatest achievement of our team of '28.

The Varsity Squad

THE TEAM

DeShazo, (Captain) . . . . *Forward*
Tanner . . . . *Forward*
Wilkins . . . . *Jumping Center*
Sinclaire . . . . *Side Center*
Winn . . . . *Guard*
Burke . . . . *Guard*
Duke . . . . *Guard*

Virginia Harper, *Manager*

The Season's Results

William and Mary	37;	Medical College of Virginia	10
William and Mary	34;	Sweet Briar	20
William and Mary	34;	Lynchburg College	23
William and Mary	26;	Adelphi	15
William and Mary	30;	New York University	28
William and Mary	29;	George Washington U.	26

TRACK TEAM

BASEBALL SQUAD

306

PROGRESS NUMBER

Advertisements

Index to Advertisers

PROGRESS NUMBER

PROGRESS NUMBER

PROGRESS NUMBER

PROGRESS NUMBER

PROGRESS NUMBER

PROGRESS NUMBER

PROGRESS NUMBER

PROGRESS NUMBER

PROGRESS NUMBER

PROGRESS NUMBER

Equipped with many years experience for making photographs of all sorts desirable for illustrating College Annuals. Best obtainable artists, and the capacity for prompt and unequalled service.

Photographers to

"1928" COLONIAL ECHO"

220 West 42nd Street   NEW YORK

PROGRESS NUMBER

The satisfaction of a service well performed is the only lasting recompense of industry.

The Canton Engraving and Electrotype Co.
Canton, Ohio
Producers of the Engravings in this Book.

The above illustration is the McKinley Memorial erected at Canton, Nineteen hundred six.

PROGRESS NUMBER

Jokes

Soph: "What is a definition for a college professor?"
Junior: "A man who is paid to study sleeping conditions among students."

* * *

Professor Bailey (in physics class): "Mr. Porter, what's a conductor for electricity?"
Porter (awakening): "Why er—er."
Professor Bailey: "Correct."

* * *

Hell hath no fury like a woman corned.

* * *

A traffic light
    Means "Stop" when red;
But lips that are
    Mean "Go ahead."

* * *

Ganter: "How did Mac come out at the handsome man contest at the college ball?"
Barrett: "He won by a bare majority."
Ganter: "I knew he'd get the coed's vote."

* * *

Mac O'Ferrall: "Dauba, do you know that every man has to start at the bottom of his business and work up?"
Dauba: "I can't."
Mac: "Why?"
Dauba: "Because I am going to be a well digger."

* * *

Pat Patterson: "Say, Milton, why is an old maid like a bad lemon."
Milton White: "Give it up."
Pat: "Because neither is worth a squeeze."

* * *

Francis Thomson: "Jack's heart is in the right place."
Charlotte: "What makes you say that?"
Francis: "Because he laid it at my feet yesterday."

* * *

Soph: "Have you heard that Sadie is engaged?"
Senior: "No, who's the plucky man?"

PROGRESS NUMBER

THIS BOOK PRINTED BY BENSON

LARGEST COLLEGE ANNUAL
PUBLISHERS IN THE WORLD

HIGHEST QUALITY WORKMANSHIP
SUPERIOR EXTENSIVE SERVICE

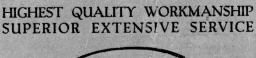

BENSON
PRINTING CO.
NASHVILLE,
TENN.

COLLEGE ANNUAL HEADQUARTERS